Educating the Other

Master Classes in Education Series

Series Editors: John Head, School of Education, Kings College, University of London and Ruth Merttens, School of Teaching Studies, University of North London

Working with Adolescents: Constructing Identity
John Head *Kings College, University of London*

Testing: Friend or Foe? The Theory and Practice of Assessment and Testing
Paul Black *Kings College, University of London*

Doing Research/Reading Research: A Mode of Interrogation for Education
Andrew Brown and Paul Dowling *both of the Institute of Education, University of London*

Educating the Other: Gender, Power and Schooling
Carrie Paechter *School of Education, The Open University*

Master Classes in Education Series

Educating the Other: Gender, Power and Schooling

Carrie F. Paechter

 The Falmer Press

(A member of the Taylor & Francis Group)
London • Washington, D.C.

UK   Falmer Press, 1 Gunpowder Square, London, EC4A 3DE
USA   Falmer Press, Taylor & Francis Inc., 1900 Frost Road, Suite 101,
           Bristol, PA 19007

© C.F. Paechter 1998

First published in 1998

**A catalogue record for this book is available from the British
Library**

ISBN 0 7507 0774 7 cased
ISBN 0 7507 0773 9 paper

**Library of Congress Cataloging-in-Publication Data are available on
request**

Jacket design by Caroline Archer

Typeset in 11/13pt Garamond and printed by
Graphicraft Typesetters Ltd., Hong Kong.

Contents

Series Editors' Preface   ix

Acknowledgments   xi

1   Introduction   1

2   Who or What Is the Other?   5
    Woman as Other   7
        The Gaze   9
    The Female as Other in Education   11
        The History of Women's Education   11
        Reason and Moral Development   14
        Male as Subject: The Gaze Is on the Girls   15
    Summary: Key Points   16
    Further Reading   17

3   Gender Differences in School   19
    Life in School   20
        Male Domination of Space and Time   20
        Male Domination of Classroom Talk   24
        Girls' Resistance to Male Domination   26
    Subject Takeup in Secondary Schools   27
    Assessment, Achievement and Examinations   31
    Deficit Models and the Schooling of Girls   34
    Summary: Key Points   35
    Further Reading   36

4   Gender as a Social and Cultural Construction   38
    Introduction   38
    Issues of Biological Sex   40
    The Development of Gendered Identities and Roles   43
    The Construction of Gender and Gender Roles in
    Western Society   45
        Gender as Dimorphic   46
        Gender Roles Involve a Power Relation   48
        Compulsory Heterosexuality   50
    Summary: Key Points   51
    Further Reading   52

5   Reconceptualizing Gender Issues in Education   54
     Introduction   54
     Power/Gender   55
     Gender, Power, Pedagogy and the Learning Child   57
     Conclusion   61
     Summary: Key Points   62
     Further Reading   63

6   Revaluing Female Voices   64
     Challenging the Mastery of Reason   64
     Reason and the Discourse of Empowerment   66
     Challenging Reason: Gender and Moral Development   71
     The Implications of Gilligan's Work for Education   75
     Summary: Key Points   78
     Further Reading   79

7   Some Voices Are More Equal than Others: Subject and
     Other in the School Curriculum   80
     Design and Technology and Physical Education:
       Life in a Marginal Subject   81
     Gendered Subject Ideologies and the Social Control
       of the Working Classes   82
     D&T and PE as Low Status Subjects   85
     Students and Subjects as Parallel Others   89
     Summary: Key Points   91
     Further Reading   92

8   Subordinated Femininities and Masculinities in
     Secondary Schools   93
     Introduction   93
     Subordinated Masculinities   93
     Sporty Girls   99
     Lesbians and Gay Males in School   103
     Summary: Key Points   107
     Further Reading   107

9   Strategies: A Toolkit   109
     'Traditional' Gender Monitoring   109
       Collating quantitative evidence   109
       Examining curriculum materials   110
       Classroom observation   110
     Examining the Relationship between Space and Power   111
       Classroom plans   111
       Staffroom plans   111
       Access to virtual space   112
     Deconstruction: What-if-Not?   113

Summary	114
Further Reading	114
10 Conclusion	115
Bibliography	118
Index	131

For Pip

Series Editors' Preface

It has become a feature of our times that an initial qualification is no longer seen to be adequate for life-long work within a profession, and programmes of professional development are needed. Nowhere is the need more clear than with respect to education, where changes in the national schooling and assessment system, combined with changes in the social and economic context, have transformed our professional lives.

The series, *Master Classes in Education*, is intended to address the needs of professional development, essentially at the level of taught masters degrees. Although aimed primarily at teachers and lecturers, it is envisaged that the books will appeal to a wider readership, including those involved in professional educational management, health promotion and youth work. For some, the texts will serve to up-date their knowledge. For others, they may facilitate career reorientation by introducing, in an accessible form, new areas of expertise or knowledge.

The books are overtly pedagogical, providing a clear track through the topic by means of which it is possible to gain a sound grasp of the whole field. Each book familiarizes the reader with the vocabulary and the terms of discussion, and provides a concise overview of recent research and current debates in the area. While it is obviously not possible to deal with every aspect in depth, a professional who has read the book should be able to feel confident that they have covered the major areas of content, and discussed the different issues at stake. The books are also intended to convey a sense of the future direction of the subject and its points of growth or change.

In each subject area the reader is introduced to different perspectives and to a variety of readings of the subject under consideration. Some of the readings may conflict, others may be compatible but distant. Different perspectives may well give rise to different lexicons and different bibliographies, and the reader is always alerted to these differences. The variety of frameworks within which each topic can be construed is then a further source of reflective analysis.

The authors in this series have been carefully selected. Each person is an experienced professional, who has worked in that area of education as a practitioner and also addressed the subject as a researcher and theoretician. Drawing upon both pragmatic and the theoretical aspects of their experience, they are able to take a reflective view while preserving a sense of what occurs, and what is possible, at the level of practice.

Educating the Other

This book addresses a central concern within education. It is a characteristic of human thought that we have to divide our experience and subsequent understanding of the world into categories or classes. Without this facility we cannot organize knowledge and, in so doing, learn from experience. But we then tend to go further and attach values to various categories. Some things are good, pleasant or desirable, while others are the reverse. Some people are like ourselves, with whom we can readily feel empathy, while some are the Other, who may be difficult to understand and may present a threat.

Within schooling this issue of the categorization of the learners runs through debates about abilities, race, class and gender. It underpins discussion about co-education or single sex schooling, streaming, selection and different-iation. At some levels, for example within higher education, we are all likely to accept the case that different groups of students should pursue a different curriculum. Within primary and secondary education the arguments are more balanced. Should, for example, pupils with Special Educational Needs be taught within different schools, or in separate classes within a conventional school, or within the ordinary classes with the provision of some extra support? The educational and social consequences of each option need to be examined.

By far the most extensive, detailed and sophisticated analysis of this process of categorization, with the subsequent classification of some as the Other, comes from feminism. It is therefore pertinent to include a feminist account of gender differentiation within this series of books on education. The importance of this topic is that it not only addresses the major concern that girls and women have been disadvantaged in many different ways, but, by analogy, helps us understand the position of other groups of students within our society.

Dr Carrie Paechter has written a scholarly but accessible account of the gender issues within education which has relevance to us all in our professional concerns.

John Head and Ruth Merttens
Series Editors

Acknowledgments

In researching and writing this book I have had both academic and personal support from a number of people. John Head and Ruth Merttens have acted as critical and supportive editors, helping me to clarify both my ideas and the ways I have expressed them. Several friends and colleagues have encouraged and helped me, both while I was developing the ideas that underlie the book and during the writing of it, by discussing ideas, suggesting further reading and commenting on drafts. I should particularly like to thank Krzysztof Blusz, Anna Craft, Gill Dawson, Dorothy Faulkner, Morwenna Griffiths, Julie Melia, Patricia Murphy, Rachel Rose, Ravi Sawney, Joan Swann, Fulden Underwood, Mel Wraight, Gaby Weiner and the members of the ESRC seminar series: *Gender and Education: Are Boys Now Under-achieving?* I am grateful also to the teachers involved in the empirical study reported in Chapter 7 and quoted in Chapters 8 and 9, who, despite the pressures of their work, gave freely of their time to participate in my research. Finally, many many thanks to Pip Eastop, who read and discussed it all and continues to be an unfailing source of encouragement.

Chapter 1

Introduction

The good constitution of children initially depends on that of their mothers. The first education of men depends on the care of women. Men's morals, their passions, their tastes, their pleasures, their very happiness also depend on women. Thus, the whole education of women ought to relate to men. (Rousseau, 1979, p. 365)

This book is about what happens to girls and young women in school and how we might go about intervening in this. Despite improvements in girls' relative academic success at the school leaving level, and despite suggestions in the press that boys are the new underachievers, girls remain second-class citizens in education and beyond.

As to the question 'Is the future female?' there is little evidence to suggest that this is the case. The possibility that women may be genuinely *equal* to men still appears to be enormously threatening. Rather the fact that we are asking this question at all suggests that current hegemonic educational discourses which seek to emphasise male underachievement might be seen as constituting a backlash to past feminist gains. What we may be seeing is, in fact, merely a new rendition of the old patriarchal refrain. (Weiner et al., 1997, p. 629)

My intention in this book is to show how and why girls' education remains subordinated to that of boys, and to demonstrate how this analysis can be used as a basis for investigating the position of other subordinated groups. Drawing on a long tradition of feminist writing, I investigate the position of girls and young women, in school and in the wider contexts in which they live. I show how a discourse in which they are positioned as Other, secondary to the all-important male Subject, disadvantages them and sidelines their needs. In the pages that follow, I shall explore how the traditions of Western society and thought have acted against the interests of girls and young women, discounting their successes and positioning them as intellectually inferior. This is particularly the case in the school context, where an emphasis on masculine forms of achievement sets girls up for a lifetime in which they struggle to break the 'glass ceilings' of education and employment. At the same time, my aim is to show how feminist writing can provide the means by which a wider variety of inequities can be analysed. Whilst my focus is girls and young women, they are not my sole concern.

In this book I talk a lot about the hegemonic nature of discourses. Both 'hegemony' and 'discourse' are important concepts, and I need to clarify my use of them. By discourse I mean a way of speaking, writing or thinking which incorporates particular things as given, unchallengeable truths. The unchallengeable nature of these 'truths' means that, within a particular discourse, only certain things can be said or thought; to question these assumptions is to step outside the discourse. Or to put it another way:

> [I am] using the term 'discourse' to refer to socially organised frameworks of meaning that define categories and specify domains of what can be said and done. (Burman, 1994, p. 2)

Discourses are useful and important; we do need to be able to set limits on what can and cannot be said within a particular context. Scientific discussion, for example, would be far more difficult if the discourse of science did not impose some restriction on what does and what does not 'count' as scientific thought. The danger, however, is that we forget that they are, simply, discourses, convenient conventions for the exchange of ideas or the carrying out of social roles, and treat them as self-evident truths. As will become clear later in the book, there are a number of educational discourses, for example, those of female academic deficit or of natural child development, that have become pernicious in this way. They have become so taken-for-granted, so unchallengeable, that they mask other ways of looking at education, and, in the process, deny girls and young women equity in this arena. Consequently, much of the book is taken up with the deconstruction of such discourses, in looking for and challenging the unquestioned assumptions underpinning them.

This deconstruction process can be difficult because of the hegemonic nature of most of the discourses under discussion. Hegemony is a concept originating in the work of the Italian socialist Gramsci (1971), which has since been applied in a variety of theoretical and practical contexts, both within and beyond its Marxist roots. It is a concept;

> designed to explain how a dominant class maintains control by projecting its own particular way of seeing social reality so successfully that its view is accepted as common sense and as part of the natural order by those who in fact are subordinated to it. (JAGGAR, A. (1983) *A Feminist Politics and Human Nature*, Sussex: Harvester Press, quoted in Lewis, 1990, p. 474)

Hegemony is thus inherent in social practices, forming part of the 'thinking-as-usual' (Schutz, 1964) of individuals within a particular society. It determines which discourses are most binding; hegemonic discourses are those which, while remaining unquestioned and often partially benign, at the same time act as forces in the oppression of some of those whose thought and behaviour they govern. Although hegemonic forces are non-cohesive, and therefore have constantly to be fought for if they are to be maintained (Giroux, 1981), they operate on individuals and groups in such a way as to make them the agents of their own oppression; for example, girls who believe in the discourse of female deficit in mathematics are likely to give up trying to succeed in that subject at an early age (Burton, 1989; Landau, 1994), thus perpetuating the power of the discourse.

Hegemony works to perpetuate the *status quo* by affecting the structures within which people think, so that they find it difficult or impossible to conceive of things in any other way. Such discourses are effective in supporting prevailing power relations because they serve to mask conflict and, as Lukes points out, 'the most effective and insidious use of power is to prevent . . . conflict arising in the first place' (Lukes, 1974, p. 23). This masking of the power of hegemonic discourses allows for the production of self-disciplining 'docile bodies' (Foucault, 1977, 1978; Smart, 1986) and the maintenance of the prevailing social order without force.

My aim in this book is to challenge some of the hegemonic discourses which structure the ways in which the education of girls and young women has been approached, while at the same time showing how this challenge can be extended to the treatment of other oppressed groups. The book is, therefore, in many ways an act of deconstruction. My intention is to use the concept of woman as Other, as a deviation from the 'normal' male Subject of discourse, to question much of what is taken for granted in the education of girls. In the first section of the book I begin this process by focusing broadly on the position of women and girls both in society as a whole and in the education system. In Chapter 2, I explain my key analytical concept, that of woman as Other, and show briefly how it can be applied to the position of girls in education. I then go on, in Chapter 3, to consider the evidence about the relations between males and females in school, suggesting that, contrary to recent popular belief, the interests of girls remain secondary to those of boys in this context. Chapter 4 considers the social construction of gender. Here I look at the evidence for how gender identities and roles come to be established in Western society and suggest that this is almost entirely the result of social rather than 'natural' forces. In Chapter 5 I set the scene for the rest of the book, by discussing the nature of gender/power relations and showing how deconstructionist analysis can call into question fundamental assumptions about the nature and methods of schooling.

The second half of the book considers three specific examples in which the female Other is reflected in ways of thinking about particular groups in the education system. Chapter 6 considers the hegemony of the discourse of reason and rationality and suggests that we need to recognize and value alternative, female voices operating within other discourses. In Chapter 7 I extend the metaphor of Otherness and consider which subjects are the Other of the school curriculum, noting in particular the relationship between their marginalization and their gendered nature. Chapter 8 focuses on three groups from the school population inhabiting subordinated masculinities and femininities: non-macho males, 'sporty' girls, and lesbians and gay men. Here I consider some of the issues around negotiating and living such identities within a context in which they are at best marginal and at worst excluded from the discourse.

Chapter 9 could easily have become a book in itself. In it I briefly outline some strategies for deconstructing and intervening in the dominant discourses of school. Finally, in the Conclusion, I summarize my position and point the way forward.

Writing this book has, for me, been a fascinating journey of exploration and discovery. I hope you find it even one-tenth as interesting as I did.

Chapter 2

Who or What Is the Other?

A man never begins by presenting himself as an individual of a certain sex; it goes without saying that he is a man. The terms *masculine* and *feminine* are used symmetrically only as a matter of form, as on legal papers. In actuality the relation of the two sexes is not quite like that of two electrical poles, for man represents both the positive and the neutral, as is indicated by the common use of *man* to designate human beings in general; whereas the woman represents only the negative, defined by limiting criteria, without reciprocity. . . . She is defined and differentiated with reference to man and not he with reference to her; she is the incidental, the inessential as opposed to the essential. He is the Subject, he is the Absolute — she is the Other. (De Beauvoir, 1949, pp. 15–16)

As women, we may share certain experiences of sexism and domestic responsibility and we may differ in ethnic origin, class or culture; but what unites most of us is our consciousness that it is other people who set the agenda. Thus what serves to link less powerful social groups are their experiences of 'otherness' and exclusion from the sites of power and meaning-making. (Weiner, 1994, p. 7)

It seems to be a general feature of human nature that we divide ourselves into in-groups and out-groups (Harbsmeier, 1985; Said, 1978). This process is partly necessary in coming to a sense of personal identity. In order to have a sense of who I am, I need to have some concomitant idea of who I am not. This has its origins in very early life as infants learn to differentiate between themselves and the rest of the world and, in particular, between themselves and their mother or other primary carer. A very important early learning experience is the difference between me and not-me. This clearly necessary distinction seems to be continued throughout life, and is an important part of the way societies are structured (Lloyd and Duveen, 1992).

This tendency to divide the world into categories of me and not-me is not, however, just a simple question of personal identity. The key issue in the creation of in-groups and out-groups is the asymmetrical power relation between them (Said, 1978). The in-group not only has the wherewithal to, as Weiner says, 'set the agenda'; it is also able to behave as if it were the *only* group, or at least the only group that matters. This is because this sort of discourse only has one positive term; the alternative, the not-me, is defined negatively as what is other than the central figure, myself. Similarly, the in-group and its members become the Subject of the discourse; the out-groups become the Other[1], that which is outside the discourse. The subject is defined in opposition to and through the exclusion of the Other; this means, paradoxically, that without that which is denied, the Other, there can be no Subject. The Other is, as a result, simultaneously feared, loathed and desired, which is why the Subject/Other relationship contains so much power. Furthermore, because of the hegemonic function of discourse, this order of things is so taken for granted that neither Subject nor Other is able to recognize the asymmetrical nature of this power relation.

In the Introduction I outlined how hegemonic forces operate in such a way as to make relations of domination and oppression appear normal and inescapable, as if things could be no other way. The language we use is particularly important in this process. Language is an important mechanism for structuring thought. This means that if our language is part of a discourse in which particular groups are treated as Other, then our thinking will focus on the dominant group, the 'taken-for-granted' subject of the discourse, and the Other will be treated as a deviant and subsidiary case. This may be limiting in all sorts of ways, for both the Subject and the Other.

What I mean by this may be made clearer by looking at an example. Morgan (1972) suggests that thinking in evolutionary theory has been seriously impeded by the dual use of the term 'man' to refer both to the human species and to the male of that species. She argues that as a result a large proportion of the work in this area is androcentric, or male-oriented:

> It's just as hard for man to break the habit of thinking of himself as central to the species as it was to break the habit of thinking of himself as central to the universe. He sees himself quite unconsciously as the main line of evolution, with a female satellite revolving round him as the moon revolves around the earth . . . Most of the books forget about [woman] for most of the time. They drag her onstage rather suddenly for the obligatory chapter on Sex and Reproduction, and then . . . get on with the real meaty stuff about the Mighty Hunter with his lovely new weapons and his lovely new straight legs racing across the Pleistocene plains. Any modifications in her morphology are taken to be imitations of the Hunter's evolution, or else designed solely for his delectation. (pp. 9–10)

So a discourse in which male is Subject and female Other can be an impediment to the development of theory. But this is not the only, nor the most pernicious, effect of treating as Other a particular group.[2] Duncan, a geographer, notes the ways in which assumptions about the centrality and superiority of one's own socio-cultural group can affect how one regards and treats those from other cultures. Positioning an alternative way of living as Other allows it to be described as 'primitive' and for people who live this way to be treated as less than fully human, as being at an earlier evolutionary stage (Harbsmeier, 1985). Spatial and cultural difference are by this means transmuted into temporal and developmental/evolutionary difference. Duncan (1993) notes, for example, that in nineteenth century Europe:

Difference was increasingly converted into history and history explained in terms of evolution. The prestige of Darwin's theory of evolution and Spencer's theory of social evolution seemed to lend renewed vigour to the age-old propensity to temporalize the Other. The tremendous interest in origins promulgated by Darwin increased the desire of Europeans to represent other people as shedding light on how Europeans' ancestors had once lived. . . . These taxonomic reforms were instituted within Britain during its age of imperial expansion. Accordingly, the new representational taxonomy had implicit political content and thus political consequences. For example, Europe was seen as the highest stage in evolution, while societies in Asia and Africa were thought to occupy progressively lower stages in the process. Evolutionary theory then provided a racist taxonomy which justified imperialism, for 'backward' places could not be expected to govern themselves. Evolutionary theory was put to creative use in the service of imperialism. (p. 46)

In this case, the treating of non-Western cultures as Other allowed imperialist nations to justify their behaviour in terms of the need to bring 'more primitive' nations to their own supposed level of civilization (Derrida, 1974). Similarly, Said traces the ways in which Western positioning of Arabs and Islam as Other in the discourse of Orientalism both contains and represents, in a series of dominating frameworks, the perceived threat of the Orient and Oriental.

The Oriental is irrational, depraved (fallen), childlike, 'different'; thus the European is rational, virtuous, mature, 'normal'. (Said, 1978, p. 40)

This conversion of 'different' into 'inferior', 'at an earlier stage of development' or exotic/erotic is common in discourses of the Other, particularly those in which the Other is female, as we shall see later.

Woman as Other

There is a line in an old folk song that runs: 'I called my donkey a horse gone wonky'. Throughout most of the literature dealing with the differences between the sexes there runs a subtle underlying assumption that woman is a man gone wonky; that woman is a distorted version of the original blueprint; that they are the norm, and we are the deviation. (Morgan, 1972, p. 7)

Who is the Other at any given place and time depends of course on who is being defined as the Subject. There are innumerable Others, as there are innumerable sets of power relations between groups, and many people experience Otherness in multiple and sometimes conflicting ways. A black lesbian, for example, will, in thinking about and resisting her Otherness, prioritize her gender, race or sexual orientation at different times and in different contexts; she may also be treated as Other as a result of any or all of these aspects of herself, even by those (for example, white women) who are Othered in some of the same ways (Carby, 1997; hooks, 1982). The same individual (for example, a white gay man) may be, in different aspects of his or her social identity, both Subject and Other (Ang-Lygate, 1996; Coyle, 1996), and different forms or aspects of a person's Otherness may cut across each other in problematic ways (Aziz, 1997; Ellsworth, 1989). In this book, however, I am going to focus in particular on the female Other, though I will draw parallels between her situation and that of alternative Others from time to time. This emphasis stems from two main sources. The first is my own position. Although I am and have been Other in a number of ways (I am the daughter of a Jewish refugee; I have a lesbian mother and stepmother) my most constant experience of Otherness has been as a woman; in writing about the female Other I am able to draw on my own experience, and, as it were, write from the heart as well as the intellect. At the same time, while not wanting to discount alternative sources, I believe that some of the most important thinking and writing on Otherness has come from feminism; it is partly to do justice to this feminist legacy that the female Other will have most of my attention in this book.

Woman has most particularly been positioned as Other because of the dualistic tradition of Western philosophical thought. This tradition looks at the world through a series of dichotomous pairs: mind/body, reason/emotion, public/private (Young, 1990). The terms in these pairs are, however, not equivalent; one is given priority over the other and, in some cases, as in the distinction between reason and emotion, one is defined simply as the negative of the other (Collins, 1990). Dichotomies such as these have long been used to distinguish Subject from Other, and to call the Other's humanness into question. For example, Duncan (1993) points out that the Hellenistic Greeks used the term *barbaros* to refer to a non Greek-speaking Other, who, because the Greeks linked intelligible speech to reason, was seen as non-rational and thus less than fully human.

Central to our discussion here, however, is that one of the most important of these dichotomies is man/woman. The other pairs are then lined up beneath them, with all the positive attributes on the male side (Lloyd and Duveen, 1992). Thus, for example, Western philosophy values reason (seen as male) over emotion (female) (Connell, 1995), and sets great store by the ability of the mind (male) to transcend the body (female) (Spelman, 1982). In a discourse in which everything is either/or, then to be male is to be rational, concerned with the mind and active in civil society, while to be female is to be emotional, concerned with the body and passively waiting at home.

Man for the Field and Woman for the Hearth:
Man for the Sword and for the Needle She:

Man with the Head and Woman with the Heart:
Man to command and Woman to obey;
All else confusion.
(Tennyson, *The Princess*, 1847, quoted in Pollock, 1988, p. 122)

Gatens (1991) suggests that, from the seventeenth century onwards, conceptions of human nature assumed the existence of a unitary and rational subject. However, two different kinds of subject were constructed: one that was apparently sexually neutral but actually male, together with a 'shadow' conception of a female subject. Unlike the rational male, whose thought could transcend worldly contingencies, this female subject remained confined by place, time, body and passion (Foucault, 1978), in short, by her gender. Because reason is associated with the male, emotion with the female, the dichotomous nature of the discourse places woman outside the reach of reason and thus outside of civil society (Heckman, 1990). She is seen as being unable to escape or transcend her body, and thus as incapable of operating on a purely rational plane (French, 1994). Because of her emotional, sexual and embodied nature, woman is regarded as being unable to operate fully in the realms of mind and reason and so cannot have complete participation in civil society. Instead, she is expected to act as a channel through which her male partner can retain some ties to nature.

> Men will philosophize about the human heart better than she does; but she will read in men's hearts better than they do. It is for women to discover experimental morality, so to speak, and for us to reduce it to a system. Woman has more wit, man more genius; woman observes, and man reasons. (Rousseau, 1979, p. 387)

Given that participation in civil society is a fundamental human function, the mind/body, reason/emotion dichotomy calls into question the very humanness of women under this discourse. Indeed, given that it was only in the twentieth century that women in the West acquired full civil rights, it might even be argued that until recently they have been regarded as not quite fully human. Differences between males and females are treated not as just alternative ways of being. The dichotomous nature of Enlightenment discourse positions men as human, as Subject, and women as Other (Woolf, 1938).

The Gaze

One context in which the relationship between male Subject and female Other is particularly exposed is in the operation of the 'gaze'. The gaze is a particular way of looking: one that is detached, dispassionate and, at the same time, powerful. The gaze contains within it a power/knowledge relation that confers, through its exercise, power to the gazer with respect to that which is gazed upon. Its detachment implies that through it the gazer can come to some sort of 'truth' about the nature of its object (Foucault, 1963). The gaze is a particularly important concept in the construction of the Other because of its objectification of that upon which it looks and because of the asymmetry of the power relation it contains (Berger, 1972). Foucault (1977) describes how the known but unseen gaze can be used as a mechanism of discipline for those to whom it is directed. If you know that a disciplinary authority is watching you some of the time, but don't know precisely when, you are forced to modify *all* your behaviour to conform to the demands of the watcher. The knowledge that 'Big Brother is watching you' constrains all of your behaviour, and the gaze becomes internalized. At the same time, the gaze, and in particular the medical gaze, was developed in the nineteenth century as a source and master of truth (Foucault, 1963); one of its objects was the feminine body, which was analysed as being saturated with sexuality (Foucault, 1978).

This process, and its effect on women, is described succinctly by Berger (1972):

> *men act* and *women appear*. Men look at women. Women watch themselves being looked at. This determines not only most relations between men and women but also the relation of women to themselves. The surveyor of woman in herself is male: the surveyed female. Thus she turns herself into an object — and most particularly an object of vision: a sight. (p. 47)[3]

The use of the gaze to construct women and their bodies in particular and sexualized ways is evident in the male-dominated traditions of Western art. Pollock points out that a key concept in the construction of the Impressionist artist (working in the period immediately following the development of the medical gaze) was the '*flâneur*', who moved through the city 'observing but never interacting, consuming the sights through a controlling but never acknowledged gaze' (Pollock, 1988, p. 67). Not only was (and is) such free movement about the city not open to women, but women themselves became the prime objects of this gaze, which is particularly intrusive, erotic and voyeuristic (Massey, 1994). Pollock contrasts the depiction of working-class women by Degas and Manet, for example, with paintings by women artists of the period such as Mary Cassatt:

> The ways in which working-class women were painted by Cassatt . . . involve the use of class power in that she could ask them to model half-dressed for the scenes of women washing. None the less they were not subject to the voyeuristic gaze of those women washing themselves made by Degas, which . . . can be located in the maisons-closes or official brothels of Paris. (pp. 88–9)

There are not only differences in the subjects of the paintings by male and female artists of this period. As important is the gaze implicit in the ways in which the women in paintings such as Manet's *A bar at the Folies-Bergère* and *Olympia* are presented to the viewer. As Pollock points out:

> To recognize the gender specific conditions of these paintings' existence one need only imagine a female spectator and a female producer of the works. How can a woman relate to the viewing positions proposed by either of these paintings? Can a woman be offered, in order to be denied, imaginary possession of Olympia or the barmaid? Would a woman of Manet's class have a familiarity with either of these spaces [the bar, the brothel] and its exchanges which could be evoked so that the painting's modernist job of negation and disruption could be effective? (p. 53)

What has all this got to do with education? Rather more than you might at first think. The construction of women both as embodied, non-rational beings and as objects of the supposedly dispassionate power-relation of the gaze has important ramifications for the way girls and women are able to function in educational institutions. The next section serves to outline how this works and to introduce the rest of the book.

The Female as Other in Education

All the influences described above feed into the construction of the female as Other within education. The female as Other in this context can be regarded both as an exemplar and as a special case of the ways in which women and girls have been constructed as Other throughout Western society. In this section I am going to develop my theme by considering in outline a number of examples of the ways in which the Othering of females has affected and been reflected in the ways in which their education has been approached. The ideas introduced here will be developed more fully later in the book.

The History of Women's Education

In the history of the education of women and girls can be found a number of themes. First, the schooling of females has been seen until very recently as being of secondary importance to that of males, and has been developed in a way which both shadows and holds up a feminized mirror to a masculine-centred education system. This is reflected even in the language used; in the US female students in co-educational institutions are referred to as 'co-eds', suggesting that the males are those at whom the courses are primarily aimed. Second, education for girls has been developed in gender-specific ways which have in many cases disadvantaged girls by excluding them from particular forms of knowledge, if only by taking up their time with other, less powerful, forms. Third, attitudes to girls' education are bound up with ideas of female embodiment, so that, again until recently, education was seen as incompatible with the physical well-being of that body.

As Weiner (1994) notes, much of what is written about curriculum, and especially about curriculum history, tends to focus almost exclusively on the curriculum for males. For example, one of the earliest and most influential modern discussions of education, Rousseau's Emile (Rousseau, 1979), covers Emile's education in great detail, only considering the parallel education of Sophie late in the text, when it becomes necessary to provide Emile with a suitably educated wife (Gatens, 1991). Even then, the main intention is to provide for Emile someone who has been preserved more or less within the state of nature, educated to be subservient to her husband and to take her opinions from him; in other words, hardly educated at all.

> Every girl ought to have her mother's religion, and every woman her husband's. If this religion is false, the docility which subjects mother and daughter to the order of nature erases from God's sight the sin of this error. Since women are not in a position to be judges themselves, they ought to receive the decision of fathers and husbands like that of the Church. (Rousseau, 1979, p. 377)

Fletcher (1984) notes that the choice facing the nineteenth century pioneers of women's education was either to provide them with an education system that had originally been set up for men, or to offer an adapted, female education, which would have lower status. This decision had to be made in a context in which educating women was seen as potentially prejudicial to their health, and, in particular, to their reproductive capacity; medical authorities argued that college education for women would lead to their sterility (Dyhouse, 1978). There was a concern to protect adolescent girls from 'mental overstrain' and it was believed that 'over-educated' women would be unable to breastfeed (Dyhouse, 1976). At the same time, it was this assumed future role of wife and, in particular, mother, that to a large extent shaped nineteenth and twentieth century girls' education. Childbearing was seen as a national duty (Manthorpe, 1986), and middle class women, in particular, were educated to be better mothers, more able, for example, to oversee the education of their children.

Throughout this period, ideas about the schooling of girls were persistently influenced by ideas about the role of women in wider society (Purvis, 1985). Thus, for example, in the nineteenth and early twentieth centuries enormous emphasis was given to domestic subjects for women of all classes; it was envisaged that, in addition to their roles as wives and mothers, working class women would need to be good servants and middle class women mistresses of servants. Even the founders of the girls' public day schools, who were inspired by the conviction that girls could do the same intellectual work as boys, and that women should aspire to a definite role in life, assumed that marriage and a vocation would be mutually exclusive; Summerfield (1987), in a study of girls' secondary schooling between 1900 and 1950 found that even in those schools in which the overriding emphasis was on an academic education with university entrance as the prime aim, the girls saw themselves as being prepared for 'professional spinsterhood' rather than a combination of work and parenthood. This attitude was reinforced by the operation of a 'marriage bar' which excluded married women from some professions, such as teaching.

These trends acted together to bring about an elementary curriculum in which, in England in 1901, a girl might spend half of the time in her last year on domestic subjects. This of course led to the exclusion of other studies; boys were usually taught elementary arithmetic while the girls did needlework (Attar, 1990; Turnbull, 1987). Both the elementary and secondary curricula for girls emphasized an ideology of service; this persists up to the present day, inscribed in the practices not only of food and textile technology (Attar, 1990) but also of business subjects (Black, 1989; Keely and Myers, 1983). Summerfield (1987) argues that schools still teach girls that their main objective is preparation for a caring role, both in the home and at work, so girls are encouraged to regard themselves as a secondary, servicing, Other to men.

Meanwhile, partly in response to the attempts of middle-class women to gain access to a more academic education, the nineteenth and the first half of the twentieth century saw a long-running debate about the issue of whether there should be a specifically female curriculum. Central to this was the question of the importance of science and, to a lesser extent, mathematics for girls. Attempts to construct a specifically female science, 'domestic science', that would replace physics and chemistry in girls' secondary schools, were fiercely resisted by the heads of these schools, who wanted girls to have an education equivalent to that of boys. However, housewifery was made compulsory in English girls' secondary education from 1905, though it remained marginal in the more academic girls' schools, and from 1907 it became possible for girls to replace science with domestic science (Hunt, 1987). Meanwhile, a specifically female tradition of physical education was being developed, again with an emphasis on the ideology of motherhood, and imbued with assumptions about female sexuality and the body. The games girls played (and still play), such as hockey, were foreshortened or adapted versions of male sports, and girls remain discouraged from taking part in contact sports, even with each other, in order to 'protect' their reproductive organs, which, unlike those of the male, are in fact safely housed in the pelvis (Scraton, 1986).

Thus, it can be seen that the education of girls has, until very recently, developed in such a way as to provide a shadow version of the male curriculum from which it was adapted, providing lower-status, attenuated versions of some key subjects. Education in domesticity was used as a means to exclude many girls from the higher status forms of knowledge which might allow them to break out of the tradition whereby a female Other provides domestic and other services to a male subject.

Reason and Moral Development

It is not uncommon for research on child development to be carried out using a narrowly defined subject base, the findings from which are then treated as if they applied to all children, with no distinction of race, class, culture or gender. One example of this is Kohlberg's work on moral development. Kohlberg, a psychologist, studied the ethical thinking of eighty-four boys over a period of twenty years, and used his findings to construct a six-stage developmental process. Although he claimed that this sequence was universal, groups omitted from his original sample, particularly women, do not usually reach the higher stages, at which morality is seen in terms of universal principles of justice, and moral judgements are arrived at by the use of reason (Gilligan, 1982).

Several things are happening here. First, this is a clear case in which the male is seen as the norm, with the female as the exceptional and inconvenient Other. Kohlberg assumes that what is true for males will be true for the entire species; males are treated as representative of all humans. Second, when other groups are found not to reach the higher stages of his scheme, this is not considered a problem for the scheme, or a reason for modifying it. Indeed, Kohlberg saw female subjects as distorting his findings, and explicitly avoided using them (Hekman, 1995). He suggests that the 'lower level' of women's moral development is contingently limited by their relatively low participation in the public world. In doing this he prioritizes the values and mores of one arena over another, suggesting that the ethical decisions made in interpersonal arenas are not truly moral (Hekman, 1990). Here he provides us with another example of the process by which cultural difference is transmuted into temporal and developmental difference. Rather than suggest that there may be alternative developmental paths, leading to different ways of conceiving of morality, Kohlberg insists that the Western 'male' model is the only correct one.

This model is in itself an interesting case of the Otherness of women. According to Kohlberg, the highest stage of moral development occurs when a person conducts ethical thinking in a formal abstract manner. This, of course, reflects the emphasis given to reason in Western moral philosophy; an emphasis which has traditionally sought to position women as outside the realm of rational debate. At the same time, as Gilligan points out, the stage in development that women are usually considered to have reached is one in which 'morality is seen in interpersonal terms and goodness is equated with helping and pleasing' (Gilligan, 1982, p. 18); such traits are precisely what has traditionally constituted the 'goodness' of women; they have been educated to be experts in interpersonal relations. Women are here caught in a double bind: they are expected and educated to concentrate on personal relationships rather than detached moral judgment, yet are condemned as being at a lower developmental stage when they act in accordance with this.

Male as Subject: The Gaze Is on the Girls

Finally, I want to look briefly at two ways in which the treatment of male students as the unacknowledged Subject in schools focuses the gaze of 'experts' and others onto the girls. I am going to discuss two very different school arenas in which girls and their supposed deficiencies are put under the spotlight in this way.

The first case I want to consider is that of school science. In recent years there has been an increasing concern about girls' relationship to school science and, particularly, school physics, focusing on two issues: their generally poor performance relative to boys, and their reluctance to pursue scientific studies beyond the point at which these cease to become compulsory (Murphy and Elwood, 1997). There seems to be a general perception that there is some degree of incompatibility between girls and school science, but the focus has been almost entirely upon the girls, rather than the science (Manthorpe, 1989). This asymmetry of focus operates at a number of levels. First, there is an emphasis on improving girls' performance in areas like science and mathematics, when until very recently there has been little corresponding interest in rectifying imbalances in performance in modern languages and the humanities, at which girls perform well relative to boys, at least to age 16 (Manthorpe, 1986). Those domains in which the male-identified attributes such as reason and logic are given prominence are seen as being more important for all students. Second, in looking at the performance in and takeup of science by girls, the focus has traditionally been on the supposed deficiencies of girls, without challenging key scientific paradigms such as the centrality of decontextualized knowledge. Murphy reports, for example, that girls are more likely than boys to take account of and respond to context in carrying out science tasks; they are then assessed as performing weakly because the unwritten rules of science require decontextualization (Murphy, 1990). Despite the rhetoric of 'girl-friendly science' little is done to make even cosmetic changes to school science education and, in England and Wales, the traditional approach has now been enshrined in a national curriculum. Osborne (1990), for example, notes that despite clear evidence that alternative examples of physics applications would be of more interest to girls than those currently provided (see, for example, Jones and Kirk (1990)), this research has had little effect on the practices of science teachers or textbook writers. Furthermore, Wajcman (1991) notes that the language and symbolism of technology is masculine and that equal opportunities recommendations in this area are in effect asking women and girls to exchange aspects of their gender expression and role for a masculine version, while no concomitant 'degendering' is asked of men.

What is happening here again is that males are treated as the Subject and females as a deficient Other. When girls perform comparatively weakly in a domain which has an overwhelmingly masculine image, the 'problem' is located in them, not in the construction of the domain. This treats the way that science is constructed as uncontested; it is the women who find it difficult to conform to this paradigm, rather than the paradigm itself, who are put under a scrutinizing gaze.

A rather more direct way in which the gaze operates in the school setting is in the regulation of the sexuality of adolescent girls. Lees (1993) notes that:

> Boys at adolescence suddenly start to describe girls in terms of their body parts. A dissecting approach is often taken to women's objectified bodies . . . To consider each and every woman only from the point of view of conquest, to describe women via parts of their bodies — face, tits, ginger minge (pubic hair) — is a reflection of the sexist ways women are depicted in advertisements and popular culture. (p. 213)

This objectifying gaze serves to police adolescent girls' behaviour. Lees points out that it is vitally important for a teenage girl not to get a reputation as a 'slag', that is, someone who 'sleeps around' or is in other ways 'loose'. She describes the use of the term as being very imprecise, having a general social control function aimed at perpetuating prevailing gender relations (Draper, 1991; Mac an Ghaill, 1996). The labelling of a girl as 'slag' can depend on a number of factors, which include the way a girl dresses or behaves:

> Appearance is crucial: by wearing too much make-up; by having your skirt slit too high; by not combing your hair; by wearing jeans to dances or high heels to school; by having your trousers too tight or your tops too low. (Lees, 1993, p. 42)

Boys are not subject to this sort of disciplinary gaze and, in fact, do most of the gazing, with more or less tacit support for their controlling activities (aimed at female teachers as well as students) from male members of staff (Draper, 1991; Mac an Ghaill, 1994b; Robinson, 1992). Again, the object of the gaze is forced to police herself, her behaviour and her dress, in order to avoid being the object of derogatory labelling. That this sort of social control is so prevalent in schools reflects the Otherness of females in wider Western society.

Summary

This chapter has outlined the concept of the Other and considered the ways in which women and girls are constructed as Other in Western society and in the school setting.

Key Points

- There is a general tendency among humans, originating in early child development, to divide the world into 'me' and 'not-me'.
- An important and powerful division is between male Subject and female Other. Although there exists a multiplicity of Others, and the concept is a useful one for addressing wider inequities, woman has been most consistently positioned in this way.
- This division is perpetuated by the dualism of Western philosophical thought, and in particular of the valuing of reason (seen as male) over emotion (seen as female).
- The gaze is an important component in the construction of woman as Other.
- Education for females has historically been seen as secondary to that for males.
- Female education has only recently broken free of its aim of making women better mothers, and girls have often studied domestic subjects to the exclusion of higher status domains.
- Developmental theories have often been constructed with a male subject as norm; this has resulted in females being seen as underdeveloped deviants. This is exacerbated in Kohlberg's theory of moral development by the emphasis on reason as the highest form of moral thought.
- In schools, girls are subject to the gaze in a number of ways. These include the emphasis on girls' failure to achieve in some areas rather than on their success in others, and the tendency to see the fault as lying with the girls rather than the subject.
- Adolescent girls are also subject to a disciplinary gaze in which their sexuality is controlled by the attitude and behaviour of boys and male teachers.

Question 1
The gaze has an important function in the disciplining of a number of groups Othered in Western society. How does it operate, for example, in the Othering of young black men in school, or lesbians and gay men in public places?

Question 2
In what ways might the dualism of Western philosophical thought influence the relative value given to different subjects in the school curriculum?

Further Reading

Given the general overview presented in this chapter it is difficult to suggest further reading; many of the ideas presented here are considered in greater detail elsewhere in the book. The following, however, would allow an interested reader to follow up more general points:

GATENS, M. (1991) *Feminism and Philosophy: Perspectives on Difference and Equality*, Cambridge: Polity Press is a critical examination of the treatment of women in Western philosophy. It is quite difficult, but covers the ground in considerably more detail than there is space for in this book.

POLLOCK, G. (1998) *Vision and Difference: Femininity, Feminism and the Histories of Art*, London: Routledge, gives a fascinating account of the ways in which nineteenth and twentieth-century Western art has positioned women as Other.

WOOLF, V. (1938), *Three Guineas*, Harmondsworth-Middlesex: Penguin Books, is an eloquent and classic account of the positioning of woman as Other in the first half of the twentieth century, and remains relevant today.

Notes

1   Readers familiar with Lacan will recognize the origins of this terminology. In this book I do use some Lacanian-derived concepts, but make no claims either for Lacanian theory or for my own fidelity to his ideas.
2   It has been argued (for example, by Brown (1994) and Woolf (1938)) that there are some advantages in the position of Other, in that it allows a clearer vision of social interaction. While there is evidence that this is indeed the case, I would argue that such clarity of vision is outweighed by the disadvantages of Otherness.
3   It has been argued (e.g. Gamman, 1988; Young, 1988) that the gaze is no longer exclusively that of male upon female. I would contend, however, that despite some sites of resistance, the objectifying gaze remains predominantly masculine in nature.

Chapter 3

Gender Differences in School

> [Children] start off in the position of the barbarian outside the gates. The problem is to get them inside the citadel of civilisation so that they will understand and love what they see when they get there. (Peters, 1965, p. 107)

In some senses, all children are Other in school[1]. Officially, schooling is geared to them and their needs, but the power lies elsewhere. Their knowledge does not count; their expertise is not valued. The point of education is to get children to understand and enjoy other, more formal kinds of knowledge, to get them to abandon their common-sense theories of how the world works and to adopt those more generally agreed upon by the teachers. In school, children's time is structured and circumscribed and the spaces they may inhabit are limited, both by time and by their lack of power (Shilling, 1991). In discussing what happens to girls in school it is important to remember that they are an even more subordinate section of a group that is already positioned as Other in this setting, and that, furthermore, they are not the only group which is Othered in this way.

It is interesting that Peters, in the quotation above, describes children as being barbarians outside the citadel of civilization. The barbarian, even when referred to as a 'noble savage' is, for Europeans, the epitome of the Other, an uncivilized creature, untouched by reason and so less than fully human (Duncan, 1993). The imperative to bring the child barbarians inside the gates of the city, to introduce them to the cultural forms valued by adult society, is very strong. Concomitantly, those who, for some reason, are unable to make this move, are considered lesser beings, as deficient. In considering why some individuals find it hard to enter the gates, or to 'love what they see' when they get there, we tend to locate the failure in themselves, and do not question the way our citadel has been constructed.

Schools are structured along lines originally developed for the education of males, and, particularly as the students get older, they are dominated by men and boys. Although the teachers of young children are mainly female, most heads of primary schools are male, and this imbalance remains through secondary schooling (Arnot et al., 1996). It is most marked in higher education, where women are outnumbered by men even at the lower levels of the hierarchy. Ohrn (1993), writing about Nordic countries, notes that, in terms of the organization and content of education, as well as in terms of inter-personal relations, school becomes more masculine as one gets older: relations with teachers become more impersonal and there is a more pronounced emphasis on achievement and competition. The curriculum, particularly at secondary level, is dominated by reason and rationality, with the more highly valued subjects being the 'detached', supposedly emotion-free areas of mathematics and science (see Chapter 7). This dominance of masculine forms of knowledge and preferred social orientation positions girls and young women as the most constant Other of the education system.

In examining the Otherness of girls and women in education, we need to start by considering the evidence for this interpretation of their position. This examination of research evidence is particularly important given that, on some measures (for example in the English and Welsh Key Stage assessments) girls, particularly those who are black or working class, perform well relative to their male peers despite manifest disadvantage and discrimination (Mirza, 1997). Given the recent concern about working-class and black male disaffection and rejection of schooling, coupled with a decline in traditional areas of working-class male employment, it is important to be aware of the evidence that the interests of girls remain subordinated in the school setting. In this chapter I am going to look in detail at some of the specific ways in which females are treated as Other in education and at some of the results of this treatment. I shall start by looking at a number of gender differences regarding approaches to and experiences at school, before considering the implications, for educational thinking, of the predominant 'deficit' approach to girls and education.

Life in School

Male Domination of Space and Time

Boys and men dominate both space and time in school. Within a situation in which both are circumscribed, for students and, to a lesser extent, for teachers, males are still able to take up more space and have greater control over the use of their own and others' time. Francis (1997) found that the femininity valued by primary school girls, which emphasizes being sensible and selfless, leads them to abandon power to the boys, who position themselves, in opposition to this, as silly and selfish. Shilling (1991) argues that the 'rules' which structure patriarchal society allow boys to gain preferential access to school resources. For example, the increased freedom of movement that males have in the outside world is reflected in their ability to dominate space in academic arenas where moving about is permitted or encouraged, such as workshops and laboratories (Dixon, 1997). Furthermore, they use this assumed dominance to take charge of scarce items of equipment, even taking them away from girls already using them (Askew and Ross, 1988), so appropriating important academic resources. Draper (1991) found that because the boys in her study messed about with equipment (for example, using bunsen burners to ignite paper and pens) both genders were denied opportunities to do practical science. Randall (1987) noted that, in the Craft, Design and Technology lessons he observed, boys tended to occupy the 'action zone' around the teacher during initial practical demonstrations; this not only gives them a good view of what they are supposed to do, but also gives them more potential eye contact with the teacher, something that is important in gaining teacher attention and the opportunity to speak in class (Swann and Graddol, 1994). Boys are also particularly dominant in high-tech areas; for example they have more or less taken over extra-curricular computer clubs by developing a games-playing culture in which girls feel uncomfortable (Mac an Ghaill, 1994b; Griffiths, 1988).

Boys are also seen by teachers as being more disruptive in the classroom than girls (Crozier and Anstiss, 1995). While this results in disproportionate exclusion of males from school, it also has a number of effects on the female experience of education. Teachers' definitions of what constitutes disruption are focused around the more overt and noisy styles of disaffected boys; this leads to more time being spent on boys both inside and outside the teaching context (Potts, 1996). Crozier and Anstiss (1995) found that 'problems' concerned with boys were more likely to be given time in meetings both within school and with outside agencies, and that intervention strategies for boys were much clearer and explicitly defined than those proposed for girls. They further note that because far more boys than girls are referred on to specialist provision, this predominantly caters for boys; girls whose behaviour is causing concern may be returned to or retained in mainstream schools simply because there are insufficient suitable alternatives.

Classroom disruption is also distracting, both for the teacher and for other students. Disruptive behaviour from a few allows boys in general to claim more classroom time and attention, and often means that lessons are geared more towards boys' interests than around those of girls (Mac an Ghaill, 1994b; Spender, 1982). Riddell (1990) argues that teachers attempt to get boys to consent to their authority by allowing them control over physical space, teacher attention and lesson content. Crozier and Anstiss (1995) found that the quieter girls in particular were deeply resentful of the amount of time teachers had to spend quelling disruption when they might have been teaching:

> The girls felt that they were being held back, that the effect of disruption was that they were treated as if they were not there and they felt angry about it.
>
> I would like some more help but the teacher is having to cope with the children, they behave like children (year 11 soft[2]). (p. 41)

Furthermore, teachers' emphasis on overt forms of disruption meant that they failed to notice or deal effectively with other disruptive behaviours that girls found particularly distressing. Name-calling, by both boys and girls, was experienced by girls as being far harder to deal with or shut out than more boisterous behaviour, and was more disruptive of their learning:

> When boys are throwing things I can block them out of my mind. When they make remarks about how girls look — 'Oh god, you're fat' — they can get me angry (Year 11 soft). (p. 42)

The domination of the disruptive antics of (often only a few) boys directs the focus of teachers' attention onto this group and positions the girls, particularly those who are quiet, as Other both in terms of their learning needs and in terms of how disruption is perceived to affect them. Because the overt instructional context is seen by teachers as the key teaching and learning time, teachers focus on interruptions to this process. The more insidious, less noticeable forms of disruptive bullying, such as name-calling, that can take place while students are working quietly, are taken less seriously, even though they have significant effects on girls' abilities to concentrate and so learn.

Outside of the classroom, males again use social privilege to dominate space. Boys dominate recreational areas, where, particularly in secondary schools, they subject girls to a critical and coercive gaze, commenting on their looks and dress (Lees, 1993; Draper, 1991). Shilling (1991) notes that by playing football, which takes up a lot of space and puts those not taking part at risk of being knocked down, boys lay claim to play areas and displace other activities. He also points out that when girls play active games they tend to take up less space than do boys, and that, while girls usually walk around others' play areas, boys walk through them, thus disrupting whatever is going on. Thorne (1993) found similar gender differences in use of outdoor play areas in her study of two elementary schools in the US:

> Boys controlled the large fixed spaces designated for team sports: baseball diamonds, grassy fields used for football or soccer, and basketball courts. In Oceanside School there was also a skateboard area where boys played, with an occasional girl joining in. The fixed spaces where girls predomin- ated — bars and jungle gyms and painted cement areas for playing four- square, jump rope and hopscotch — were closer to the building and much smaller, taking up perhaps a tenth of the territory that boys controlled.

Older girls, whose social life, more than that of boys, is focused around friendships and the exchange of confidences, often have few safe areas in which they can talk; given the importance of mutual support in dealing with verbal and physical harassment, this lack is particularly keenly felt. Often the only space girls have to themselves is the lavatories, and even here they may be disturbed:

> Retreating to the girls' toilets featured as a way of claiming a private safe space, but no longer served as a haven because the boys were prone to invading them. (Crozier and Anstiss, 1995, p. 43)

Physical, and particularly, sexual harassment, clearly limits the areas in which girls feel safe. Several studies, for example, (Lees, 1993; Draper, 1991; Dixon, 1997; Crozier and Anstiss, 1995; Riddell, 1990; Lee et al., 1996) have suggested that this form of verbal and physical bullying is common in schools. Lee et al., in a nationally representative sample study in the US, found that 83 per cent of girls and 60 per cent of boys claimed to have been sexually harassed in school, usually, though not always, by their peers. Although nearly three-quarters of the victims admitted to having been perpetrators themselves at least once, girls were more likely to have been exclusively victims, and boys more likely to have been exclusively perpetrators of such harassment. The harassment described by girls was more severe, in terms of its effects on them, than that described by boys. Girls were also more likely to attempt avoidance behaviours as a strategy for dealing with the problem; these ranged from keeping away from certain individuals and areas of school to dropping out of courses, thinking about changing schools and missing school altogether. Myers and Dugan (1996) found graduate students experiencing gender bias by staff reported suffering similar academic consequences, such as steering away from particular disciplines or leaving graduate school altogether. Lee et al. (1996) argue that there are some schools where a culture of sexual harassment prevails and in which the majority of students, both girls and boys, are likely to experience it at some stage of their school lives.

Draper, who studied the amalgamation of a boys' school, a girls' school and a mixed school, found that sexual harassment of girls by boys was often tolerated by male teachers, who saw it as a natural part of boisterous adolescence. Girls who were the victims of such unwelcome sexual attentions could also find themselves being considered to have provoked them by their dress or behaviour (Mac an Ghaill, 1994b):

> The overt sexual behaviour on the part of the boys seemed to be taken for granted as 'normal' by some of the men, particularly teachers from the Boys' school.

>> You've got to understand that our boys can be a bit boisterous. They've been in an all male environment for a couple of years, and it's their way of breaking out of it. After all it's quite normal behaviour in healthy young males. (ex-Boys' School male teacher)

> However, the same teacher also said:

>> What else can you expect when you've got that type of girl in the school. (Draper, 1991, p. 9)

This discourse in which male sexual aggression is seen as a normal part of development is not confined to secondary schooling. Walkerdine and the Girls and Mathematics Unit give a vivid example in which two nursery school boys verbally harass not only another child ('You're a stupid cunt, Annie') but their teacher, through a series of overt sexual taunts which include such demands as 'Miss Baxter, show off your bum', 'Miss Baxter, show your knickers your bum off' and culminate in 'Take your teeth out, take your head off, take your hair take your bum off. Miss Baxter the paxter knickers taxter' (Walkerdine and The Girls and Mathematics Unit, 1989, pp. 65–6). The teacher's only rejoinder is to say that they are being very silly and to ask them to find something else to do; she describes their behaviour later as being normal for boys of this age. In doing so, she fails to protect the girls in the group from being subjected to abuse, and reinforces the idea in the boys that using such language to others is not an occasion for serious reprimand.

Male secondary school teachers often tacitly support a more general school atmosphere in which girls and women are positioned as sexual Others and made the object of derision (Dixon, 1997). Riddell (1990) found that some male teachers sought to maintain control in the classroom by establishing an atmosphere of male camaraderie based on sexual joking. Such joking is also common in staffrooms as a way of preserving male dominance over women teachers (Cunnison, 1989); such dominance can extend to the sexual harassment of female staff by male students (Riddell, 1990).

Male Domination of Classroom Talk

With the growth in importance of student-centred learning, classroom talk has become increasingly central to the teaching and learning process. However, girls are not given equal access to this form of learning. Luke (1994) notes that in classrooms, boys out-talk girls by a ratio of 3:1, and girls' contributions are praised less than those of boys. Language is a form of social practice (Swann, 1992), and the ways in which it is regulated and used in school both reflect and prepare students for gender inequalities in language use in wider society. Swann and Graddol (1994) note that:

> mixed sex talk among adults is often dominated by men, both in the senses that men talk more, and in the sense that men seem to control topics, interrupt women more than they are interrupted by women; use various aggressive tactics in order to get to speak, and so on . . . In other words, the inequality of talk among adults is not an incidental feature of women's reluctance to talk — it rather results from a complex social process which seems to endow men with greater power than women in social interaction. (p. 153)

Such inequalities are evident even in primary schools. Fisher (1994), for example, observed four children, two girls and two boys, aged between six and seven, working collaboratively on seven tasks. She noted that the boys dominated the talk throughout, turning their backs on the girls, speaking

mainly to each other and ignoring the girls' contribution
girls were involved in the discussion, their ideas were n
boys and girls saw the boys' ideas as more important. This
only has implications for girls having confidence in the imp
ideas, but may also lead them to gain lower ratings in teach
of their work, because they will be seen as having contribut
group solution.

Inequalities in participation are also apparent when pupils ar_ interacting with teachers. Swann and Graddol (1994) conducted a detailed analysis of teacher-student interactions during a period of class teaching in two different classrooms. They found that boys talked more than girls, in terms of the number of words uttered, the number of speaking turns they took and the number of interchanges they had with the teacher. Furthermore, such turn-taking was largely controlled by the teacher, both by naming students who had volunteered to talk by raising their hands, and by the non-verbal means of inviting someone to speak by looking at them. The gaze, Swann and Graddol (1994) argue, is an important way through which the next speaker in a conversation can be cued to begin. They found that, when talking to the class, the teacher gazed at the boys more than the girls, particularly when formulating a question, thus making it more likely that a boy would be invited to speak. This, they suggest, is partly because experienced class teachers will scan the class all the time in order to check for emerging discipline problems; the more generally boisterous behaviour of boys means that the teacher will tend to look in their direction more of the time:

> In several interchanges we found the teacher's gaze drawn towards the boys by muttering, which ensured that a boy was invited to respond. (p. 160)

This form of classroom talk can also be seen as competitive; in the rapid to and fro of teacher-student interaction it is usually the first to offer to respond (by raising one's hand or catching the teacher's eye) who gets to speak. Research on adult conversations suggests that this is a form of talk more often used by men; in women-only groups the emphasis is on co-operative talk (Swann, 1992, Tannen, 1991). By focusing on this form of interaction, teachers are not only marginalizing those less comfortable with competitive conversation but giving those who already excel in it further opportunities to develop their skills.

It would appear, then, that girls are marginalized in two forms of class-room talk that are important learning contexts: learning through collaborative discussion in mixed groups and class discussion with the teacher. This not only denies them the opportunity to work through their ideas and have them acknowledged and valued, but also gives them comparatively little experience of success in the competitive talk that often characterises mixed adult discussion, particularly in public arenas.

Girls' Resistance to Male Domination

Of course, boys' domination of school space and time does not go unresisted by girls. Girls use a number of strategies to assert their own power and prevent their marginalization. This is particularly clear at infant and nursery level, where girls have been found to use fantasy play revolving around domestic situations as a way of gaining control over boys. Because, from the point of view of the young child, women, as mothers, are very powerful in the domestic arena, girls are able to assume power by acting the role of mothers in fantasy play. Walkerdine (1990), for example, describes a scene in which a group of nursery school children have been equipped for a game of doctors and nurses. The nursery nurse has dressed all the boys as doctors and all the girls as nurses, and further underlined this power differential by asking the nurses to 'help' the doctors. Walkerdine (1990) describes how this gender/power relation is subverted by one of the girls:

> One girl, Jane, changes this into a situation where she is to make cups of tea for the patients. She goes into the Wendy House and has a domestic conversation with another girl, then the following sequence ensues: (One of the doctors arrives in the Wendy House and Jane says to him:)
>
> > *Jane*: You gotta go quickly.
> > *Derek*: Why?
> > *Jane*: 'Cos you're going to work.
> > *Derek*: But I'm being a doctor.
> > *Jane*: Well, you've got to go to work, doctor, 'cos you've got to go to hospital and so do I. You don't like cabbage, do you? [He shakes his head] . . . Well you haven't got cabbage then. I'm goin' to hospital. If you tidy up this room make sure and tell me.
>
> Jane has managed to convert the play situation from one in which she is a powerless and subservient nurse to the only one in which she has power over the doctor: by controlling his domestic life, by becoming the controlling woman in the home. (pp. 10–11)

In this situation, female resistance to male power is enacted through the playing out of traditional female roles. As children get older, however, this may no longer be possible. Teachers' differential expectations of male and female behaviour can often mean that resistance is costly to girls in a number of ways. Robinson (1992), for example, found that teachers saw girls as passive, submissive and controllable. Because they were viewed as 'fragile' they were treated more carefully than were boys, with compliance obtained by negotiation rather than the threat of violence. This expectation that girls would be well behaved did allow them to avoid working without being noticed provided they kept quiet and looked busy. Girls who are prepared to conform outwardly to their expected passive classroom roles can use this as a cover for quiet resistance. However, this brings with it the danger that they will be seen as intellectually unadventurous and as less intelligent than the boys (Walkerdine and The Girls and Mathematics Unit, 1989).

Girls who deviate from this expected behaviour, and who mount overt challenges, particularly to masculine authority, are, however, seen by teachers as discipline problems. Boisterousness, competitiveness and unruliness are considered deviant when coming from girls, although they are ignored or even praised when exhibited by boys (Robinson, 1992; Walkerdine and the Girls and Mathematics Unit, 1989; Kessler et al., 1985). Girls' challenges to teacher knowledge or questions about the relevance of the topic can lead to power battles in class, and may be seen as an affront to the masculinity of a male teacher. When this comes from boys, however, it is accepted as a normal aspect of male academic sparring (Robinson, 1992), and even treated as a sign of intelligence (Walkerdine and the Girls and Mathematics Unit, 1989). Furthermore, not only are assertive girls seen as being problematic, but their deviance is also described in particular pejorative terms. Crozier and Anstiss (1995), for example, found that in meetings to discuss problem students, while boys were usually described in terms of their behaviour and academic performance, girls tended to be described in terms of their appearance and sexuality. Girls who deviate from the expected model of quiet passivity are likely to find that both teachers and students make harsh judgments about their appearance and morals; they are described as 'tarty' (Robinson, 1992; Crozier and Anstiss, 1995), one of the worst insults that can be applied to a teenage girl (Lees, 1993; Draper, 1991).

Subject Takeup in Secondary Schools * presentation

Despite some movement towards equality of takeup of subjects post-14, it remains the case that secondary school students perceive at least some subjects as being gendered. Although the statutory requirement that all students in England and Wales take mathematics, science, English, a modern foreign language and technology (design and technology (D&T) and information technology (IT)) until the age of 16 has meant that stereotypical choices only become really noticeable later on, differences remain, both in the other subjects chosen and in choices within options. Stables and Wikeley (1996) found, for example, that although both boys and girls had to study d&t, within that overall subject, boys were more likely to opt for graphics or resistant materials and girls for food technology. Where subjects were not compulsory, boys were more likely to choose physical education (PE) and geography, girls child care/child development and French. They conclude that:

> While the opportunity for gender differentiation in this respect has been diminished, there is still evidence of some gender patterning in choices, with girls appearing to favour subjects involving direct personal interaction. (p. 8)

This suggestion that girls prefer subjects which have clearly identifiable human factors is supported by evidence from studies concerned with girls' reluctance to engage with physics and mathematics, particularly at higher levels. Walkerdine and the Girls and Mathematics Unit (1989) note not only the relative absence of female images in secondary school mathematics texts, but that often no human figures are shown at all; they argue that this does not help students to see the human applications of the subject. Even within physics, a subject largely seen by students as masculine, girls and boys have been found to be interested in different topics (Johnson and Murphy, 1986). In a study conducted in New Zealand looking at 15–16 year olds' interests in applications of school physics, Jones and Kirk (1990) found that while the main reason for students being interested in a particular device was whether it involved people, girls were more concerned about the people involved than in the actual device, and were more interested in medical examples than were boys, who were particularly engaged by new technology. Boys were also more interested than girls in finding out how things worked, while girls had a high level of interest in aesthetic examples such as rainbows. Neither group was interested in 'school physics' type examples (forces on a moving object, kinetic energy) or in industrial applications, although boys felt less strongly than girls about both of these. Jones and Kirk (1990) suggest that changing the examples used in physics teaching might increase the number of students, particularly girls, who show an interest in the subject. Similar differences were found by the Assessment of Performance Unit in the UK (Murphy, 1990). Wolffensperger (1993), who studied a group of women attending a Dutch agricultural college also found that they felt distanced from the mainly male academic staff, who used their scientific knowledge as a source of power. Women students dealt with the overwhelmingly scientific atmosphere by taking social science courses as subsidiary options, using studies of human-oriented areas to prevent themselves from dropping out of college altogether.

Students make stereotyped subject choices for a number of reasons. Peer-group pressure and the need to distinguish oneself from the other gender seem to be important factors in mixed secondary schools. Stables (1990) found that boys, in particular, were more likely to make stereotyped option choices in mixed than in single sex schools. Teachers may also collude in the formation and preservation of gendered perceptions of some subjects (Carroll, 1995). Riddell (1992) argues that in the two schools she studied subjects were presented to students in such a way as to ensure that gender boundaries remained; physics, for example, was presented as abstract and not human, while home economics (HE) courses, with the exception of pre-catering, were depicted as being to do with women's concerns. Landau (1994) found that boys were more likely to give career-related reasons for choosing mathematics A level than were girls, and often saw the perceived status and difficulty of the subject as giving a favourable impression to university admissions tutors; girls did not seem to take such things into account, and were far less career-focused. Riddell (1992), on the other hand, argues that girls', often stereotypical, option choices at age 13–14 can be seen a logical response to be perceived external circumstances, with subjects selected to prepare themselves for adult and working life in a sexist world. Girls also valued the female atmosphere of subjects like HE, where there were few boys and they felt safe from sexual harassment (Riddell, 1992).

Archer (1992) reports that 'masculine' subjects are seen as 'difficult' by girls, but 'interesting' by boys, while girls see 'feminine' subjects as 'easy' and boys see them as 'boring'. Riddell (1992) also found that both genders actively reinforced gender boundaries through their perceptions of certain subjects as being male or female; boys tended to emphasize the importance for girls of the stereotypically feminine subjects, while defending their dominance of science and technology on the grounds of mental ability and physical strength. Both girls and boys used each other as a negative reference group in the maintenance of gender boundaries; girls saw doing stereotypically male subjects such as physics as a threat to their feminine identity, and there were similar issues to be faced by boys opting for HE (Riddell, 1992). Attar (1990) found that boys studying HE had a very different attitude to it from that of girls, taking it much less seriously and treating it as a fun activity; this was reflected in teachers' lower expectations of boys' performance. At the same time, the teachers in Riddell's (1992) study encouraged boys to opt for 'girls' subjects by saying they would be better at them than the girls.

Attempts to make education more equitable by providing students of both genders with the same diet may not be the best counter to the gender stereotyping of school subjects. Unless the curriculum is carefully planned, it is likely to address male interests, with females positioned as Other and ignored. Leaman (1984), for example, notes that where physical education (PE) is taught in mixed groups it often means girls playing with boys at 'men's' games such as football and cricket, because boys are reluctant to play 'women's' games. This causes problems in skill-based lessons because boys often have more experience of these activities and thus have had more opportunity to acquire skills; Carroll (1995) speculates that the reason more girls than boys are excluded by teachers from GCSE[3] PE is that their performances, in the mixed context, are judged less favourably than those of boys. There is also a tendency, in these circumstances, for boys to dominate and get more teacher time. Because there is a cultural association between competitive activities and masculinity, the introduction of mixed PE can make lessons much more competitive, which in its turn can make girls more disaffected. Given the tendency for adolescent girls to avoid school PE in any case, this suggests that mixed PE does not serve young women well. Leaman suggests that the sidelining of girls in mixed sports and the tendency for teachers to deal with unwilling adolescent girls by providing an unchalleng-ing, recreational rather than educational PE curriculum, prepares girls for a future in which they have low physical status and little access to public leisure facilities (Leaman, 1984). This preparation for a physically inferior future starts as early as primary school, where teachers' lack of expertise in subjects like gymnastics and dance can lead to a games-dominated curriculum in which boys play high status sports, such as football, with an obvious carry-over into adult leisure activity. Furthermore, as most primary PE postholders are male, boys are more likely to be provided with extra-curricular activities than are girls (Williams, 1993).

Even where there is a reasonable degree of uniformity as regards what is taught, the masculine image of certain subjects, and the concomitant classroom atmosphere, can make girls reluctant to continue with them once they are no longer compulsory. Unfortunately, the subjects girls tend to reject as 'masculine', particularly physical science and mathematics, are those with far more social prestige than those rejected by boys, such as textile or food technology. Although girls no longer seem to be performing poorly in 'masculine' subjects, they still tend to stop studying them as soon as they can. It would seem that, to paraphrase Peters (1965), girls are being brought inside the citadel of civilization, understand what they see when they get there, but still do not love it. This applies even to girls who do particularly well in these areas. Landau (1994), for example, found that, in the two sixth form colleges she studied, boys with high grades in mathematics GCSE were more likely to take the subject on to A level[4] than were high-performing girls. They liked the competitive nature of their lessons, and saw difficult problems as challenges to be overcome. Girls, on the other hand, however successful, were put off by the competitive atmosphere in the classroom (Boaler, 1997). This seems to have been a particular problem in schools where 'express sets' were established to allow some students to take mathematics GCSE a year early. Perhaps because of teachers' reluctance to pressurise girls (Walkerdine and the Girls and Mathematics Unit, 1989), these groups were very male dominated, and the forced pace made the girls uncomfortable and sapped their confidence. For those who did not make it into the express stream, this was seen as an indication that they were not good enough to take the subject further, a belief sometimes reinforced by teachers:

> Four students had been in express groups and achieved the top grade, but their self-confidence had not benefited. Incredibly, all of them felt that they were weak mathematics students[,] commenting, 'I was like the bottom of the set the whole time', 'maths was always my hard subject that I couldn't do' and 'they were all really clever, like genius clever. I didn't think I was very good at it'. They had also suffered from the pressure imposed by the pace, and having achieved the accolade of being included in such a group, they felt obliged to keep up in a very competitive and pressurised atmosphere . . .
>
> Five students discussed how it felt being in the next group down, expected to achieve an A, but *only* at the end of year 11[5]. This provided them with proof that they were 'not good enough' and in such schools teachers were sometimes said to confirm such distortions: 'my teacher said you're

not in the top set, you can't take it' and 'they were very very good, and so you just felt the teachers didn't really expect anyone in our set to take it.' (Landau, 1994, p. 44)

On this evidence, the atmosphere of this particular citadel of knowledge does not encourage girls to enjoy their sojourn there.

Assessment, Achievement and Examinations

Despite their marginalization, girls perform comparatively well in compulsory schooling. Overall, girls in England have been more successful than boys at school-leaving examinations for some time; more girls than boys gained five or more A-C grade GCSE passes (or their CSE and O level equivalents[6]) in almost all the years between 1975 and 1995, though the gap remained slight until the 1980s, when it slowly increased. Between 1990 and 1995 this disparity in performance stabilized, with the percentage of the male cohort gaining five or more A-C grades being consistently about four-fifths of the percentage of girls achieving this level. The differences are much smaller if the percentages gaining grades A-G are compared, although girls still do slightly better. This improvement of females relative to males has not, however, been at the expense of male performance; both groups considerably improved their percentages of A-C grades in particular between 1975 and 1995 (Department for Education and Employment, 1996).

Reporting the results in terms of A-C grades, however, may mask other differences, however, as becomes clear when we examine what happens after compulsory schooling has finished, particularly at A level. In these examinations, boys outperform girls in almost all subjects (Weiner et al., 1997). Furthermore, boys gain more top grades (Murphy and Elwood, 1997). For example, in 1995, while the percentage of the male A level entry gaining grades A-C was only slightly greater than that of the female entry, only 15.9 per cent of female entries attained grade A, compared to 18.2 per cent of male entries; that is, the female grade A rate was only 87 per cent of that for males. This reflects the tendency for male students to perform at the extremes of attainment throughout schooling (Arnot et al., 1996; Gipps and Murphy, 1994); at A level, of course, those who would perform at the lower extreme are excluded in the first place.

This discrepancy between male and female students in attaining the very top scores of course results in differential life chances in terms of prestige university places, scholarships and so on. In the US, university entrance is based on standardized tests (usually the Scholastic Aptitude Test, or SAT) and scholarships are awarded in part on the basis of a preliminary test, the PSAT. Because males tend to score higher, they gain most of the 7000 National Merit Scholarships (Kleiner, 1996). These higher scores are believed to occur because males outperform females on the mathematics portion of the SAT, which is multiple-choice in format. However, when college outcomes for mathematics are compared to their original SAT score, women have a lower SAT score than males with the corresponding outcome (i.e. women do better than their scores predict), suggesting bias in the test (Gipps and Murphy, 1994). Given that girls have been found to perform less well than boys on multiple-choice questions (Gipps and Murphy, 1994), this may be an explanation for the discrepancy; meanwhile, from 1997, the PSAT includes an additional section on the correct use of written English, something at which girls are usually more successful, and which, it is hoped, will even out the overall scores (Kleiner, 1996).

In addition to performance differentials in favour of top-scoring males, there are important gender differences in examination entry at A level. In 1995, nearly four times as many males were entered for physics as females, and despite the probability that physics is only taken by girls who are particularly good at it (Murphy and Elwood, 1997), boys also achieve proportionally more A grades (23.2 per cent:19.9 per cent of the entry in 1995). There is a similar, though not so extreme, story regarding mathematics. In the same year, nearly twice as many males were entered for mathematics as were females, with 29 per cent of the male entry gaining grade A, compared with 26.4 per cent of the female entry. Even in English, where more than twice as many girls as boys were entered, the proportions in 1995 gaining grade A were 16.4 per cent males to 14.7 per cent females (Department for Education and Employment, 1996).

This variation in performance in favour of males is particularly interesting given that prior to A level girls almost consistently outperform boys overall. At school entry, girls do better than boys in all areas except gross motor skills, where differences are not significant, and this differential performance is found again at the end of Key Stage 1 (age 7). Overall, girls also achieve higher levels in the Key Stage 2 tests (age 11), although in English girls tend to perform around the mean, while boys are extreme high and low scorers (Arnot et al., 1996). This reflects earlier findings from the Assessment of Performance Unit (APU) mathematics tests, in which there were more boys in the top 10 per cent and 20 per cent and in the bottom 10 per cent cohorts (Gipps and Murphy, 1994). Furthermore, Gipps and Murphy note that, at Key Stage 1, teacher assessment also gave more boys scores at the extremes.

The tendency for girls to be regarded as average and boys as either excellent or poor can have effects in terms of whether a student gains access to higher levels of assessment at all. For example, Gipps and Murphy (1994) report that boys tend to be entered for the top and bottom (grade-limited) tiers of mathematics GCSE examinations, with girls in the middle tier; this, they suggest, reflects teachers' belief that girls are generally mediocre performers who lack confidence. Their findings are supported by earlier research which suggests that teachers restricted girls' access to higher level examinations while entering boys with comparable test scores, with girls' supposed lack of confidence under examination conditions again cited as the reason for discrimination (Walden and Walkerdine, 1985). Gipps and Murphy (1994) also point out that:

> there is evidence that some 1 per cent of students (about 5000) who were entered for the intermediate tier could have achieved a higher grade and that this affects more girls than boys. This 'misclassification' restricts their ability to continue their study of mathematics to A level. (pp. 224–5)

While performance gaps at A level are gradually narrowing, and while more females than males are gaining two or more A levels at school, there remain gender discrepancies as regards vocational qualifications. Only two-thirds as many females as males are attaining vocational qualifications at Level 2, and the gender gaps are much wider than for academic qualifications. This gap is particularly acute within Pakistani/Bangladeshi groups, although it is also substantial within the white and Afro-Caribbean populations. Only among students of Indian origin do females gain more vocational qualifications than males (Arnot et al., 1996). While girls in general do seem to be more successful at completing vocational courses than are boys, differences in course choice mean that they gain fewer qualifications of this type. Furthermore, students opt for vocational courses along traditional gender-stereotyped lines, with young women taking courses such as business and commerce and nursery nursing and young men those in construction or traditional science subjects (Arnot et al., 1996).

The situation regarding examinations and assessment is therefore complex. Where differential attainment between males and females exists, it may be due to a number of causes, including the composition of the test, differential levels of entry, and variations in course takeup. In discussing these discrepancies there has also been a clear tendency to treat females as Other, with the focus on the white male as norm. Where girls have underperformed boys, there has been a tendency to attribute this to 'natural ability', with comparative female performance being explained by differences in brain function, for example, rather than by differential educational opportunities. Where girls outperform boys, on the other hand, this is put down to males' poor motivation due to social circumstances; boys could, of course, do better if they wanted to (Weiner et al., 1997). As Gipps and Murphy (1994) point out:

> More effort has gone into exploring cognitive deficits in girls to explain their poor performance [in science] than into asking whether the reliance on tasks and apparatus associated with upper middle-class white males could possibly have something to do with it. Similarly, we feel that focusing on 'bias' in tests, which suggests that there is such a thing as a fair test, has distracted attention from wider equity issues, such as actual equality of access, inhibiting classroom practices and the like. (p. 263)

Deficit Models and the Schooling of Girls

The image of the child as the 'barbarian outside the gates' of learning (Peters, 1965) is a particularly strong force in the positioning of girls and women as Other in education. The citadel is masculine, established for the education of white middle-class young men, with females allowed to participate only comparatively recently. It is not surprising, then, that even those who are able to equip themselves to enter this male stronghold often do so reluctantly, and find it difficult to love what they see when they get there.

The discourse of the child as barbarian outside the gates of adult civilization appears on the surface to assume the equal potential for all children to enter. It appears to assume that all are capable of being civilized, of being assimilated into the cultural world of socially-valued knowledge, and that all are capable of loving it once they get there. However, it fails to take into account the differential starting points of the various candidates for entry. The implication of the discourse is that those who do not or cannot enter the citadel are deficient in some way, that those who, given the opportunity to learn, still are unable or unwilling to become full members of the educated community, have some fundamental fault. This, I argue, is what has happened to girls and women.

Because the Subject of education is male (Peters, for example, refers to males and to 'the educated man' throughout his paper), and because females are constructed as Other to the male, it is not surprising that females are seen as deficient in educational contexts. Both the learner and the educated individual that he will become are constructed as male, and females do not always fit into this model. Walden and Walkerdine (1985) argue that the active, curious, exploratory Piagetian child on whom Western primary education is founded is in fact not neutral but male; girls are encouraged to be passive by teachers, who then interpret their reluctance to challenge teacher ideas as evidence that they lack intelligence. Boys, on the other hand, are attributed high intelligence on the basis of their level of activity, rather than on the evidence of their achievement. Walden and Walkerdine (1985) also point out that girls are encouraged to be rule-following in tackling primary mathematics, and that this in fact serves them well at this level; when they get to secondary school, their learned reluctance to 'break set' and challenge procedures means that they become labeled as lacking in 'real understanding'. Girls' lack of fit with the dominant model of the enquiring learner is seen as implying intellectual weakness rather than suggesting that there might be alternative models of children's learning and development.

Burchell (1995) argues that this is further exacerbated when classroom-type judgments are incorporated into semi-public documents such as Records of Achievement (RoAs). Teachers, she notes, show differences in their perceptions of the behaviour and attitude of male and female students, for example in attributing the attainment of boys to their ability and that of girls to effort. This, combined with the tendency for boys to overestimate and girls to underestimate their performance in subjects like science (Murphy and Elwood, 1997), the increased confidence of boys in reporting their worth and their greater willingness not only to talk about themselves but also to contest negative teacher assessments, may make the RoAs of boys look much more positive than those of girls. Burchell argues that the expectations of what should go into an RoA are likely to disadvantage female students, who do not respond well to the focus in the record on active and competitive aspects of their lives. This masculine bias in the structure and content of the RoA may therefore disadvantage young women if what it contains is taken at face value by employers (Burchell, 1995).

Historically, there has been a tendency for middle-class white males to appropriate whatever are the high-status subjects at a particular time and to model them after their own image. Delamont (1994), for example, notes that, while science has an overwhelmingly masculine image today, in the nineteenth century it was considered particularly suitable for women; it was classical studies that was then seen as a male preserve. Griffiths (1988) notes the appropriation and masculinization of computer culture both inside and outside of the education system, while Massey (1995) argues that a form of rational, scientific masculinity is dominant in those (mainly males) working in high status, high-tech science industries. Having defined whatever is important in a particular society (and being able to do this because of their status as Subject), males are thus enabled to conduct that activity in such a way that it is unwelcoming to females, who may have different ways of working, for example focusing on interpersonal relations in the work group rather than on the task (Pryor, 1993). Because of their position as Other, the excluded females are then encouraged to see their lack of fit with this dominant paradigm as a lack in themselves rather than a result of the exclusionary practices of the in-group. Such an approach is exacerbated by investigations into differential performance that do not take into account prior experience in carrying out the task being assessed (Gipps and Murphy, 1994).

It would thus appear that the citadel of learning and culture is constructed in such a way that those who are to become full citizens have to think and behave in certain ways. These ways, as will become increasingly apparent throughout this book, are those of middle-class white males. The challenge is to find ways of constructing the citadel differently and more inclusively, or, alternatively, of making it possible for a variety of truly equal citadels to co-exist.

Summary

This chapter has outlined a number of ways in which girls and women are positioned as Other in education.

Key Points

- ✳● Schools are structured along lines originally developed for the education of middle-class white males and are dominated by men and boys.
- ✳● Boys and men dominate space and time in schools, both in classrooms and in recreational areas.
- ✳● Male disruptive behaviour focuses teachers' attention on boys and leads them to gear the curriculum to boys' interests while quiet girls, in particular, are ignored.
- ● Verbal and physical sexual harassment is common in schools. While both genders can be victims, sexual aggression is often seen as a normal part of male development. Female victims may be blamed for 'encouraging' abuse.
- ● Boys tend to dominate classroom talk, both in student-only groups and in discussion with the teacher.
- ● Girls use a number of strategies to assert their own power in the classroom, but these often lead to conflicts with teachers.
- ✳● Subject choices at secondary level, and especially post-16, remain gendered. Where subjects are presented as gender-neutral, they are often mainly concerned with 'male' interests and expertise.
- ✳● Despite their marginalization, girls do comparatively well at compulsory schooling. However, boys outperform girls in nearly all subjects at A level, and gain proportionately more of the top grades. This has a significant effect on future opportunities. Fewer females gain vocational qualifications, especially in some ethnic groups.
- ● Because the Subject of education is male, females are seen as deficient in educational terms. Females' lack of fit with dominant male paradigms is seen as due to personal failings, not to the exclusionary practices of
- ✳ the in-group.

Question
Recently, deficit models have been extended to working-class males, who have been seen as failing in school for a number of reasons. How does this Othering of some groups of boys relate to the continued Othering of girls within the school context?

Further Reading

DELAMONT, S. (1990) *Sex Roles and the School*, London: Routledge, gives an excellent and very readable overview of the literature on gender and schooling.

   GIPPS, C. and MURPHY, P. (1994) *A Fair Test? Assessment, Achievement and Equity*, Buckingham: Open University Press, gives a detailed account of issues of equity in assessment, with a particular focus on testing regimes in the UK and USA.

WALKERDINE, V. and THE GIRLS AND MATHEMATICS UNIT (1989) *Counting Girls Out*, London: Virago, looks at the ways that the ideologies and practices of schooling position girls as failing at mathematics. Although focused on one subject, this book has relevance across education, including nursery schooling.

THORNE, B. (1993) *Gender Play: Girls and Boys in School*, Buckingham: Open University Press, is an important source for those interested in what goes on in those parts of school beyond the classroom.

Notes

1 I am grateful to Rachel Rose for this insight.
2 The term 'soft' was used by a group of girls in the study to describe themselves. Crozier and Anstiss note that their use of this term is not intended to suggest weakness, but that members of this group took on the role of 'quiet girl' in the classroom.
3 GCSE is the normal school-leaving examination in England and Wales, usually taken at age 16.
4 Advanced level, the main university entrance examination in England and Wales, usually taken at age 18. Students normally study between two and four subjects.
5 i.e. at age 16, when it would normally be taken.
6 The English and Welsh two-tier examination system of O level and CSE was replaced in 1988 by a common examination, the GCSE. Grades A-C correspond to O level pass grades. G is the lowest GCSE pass grade.

Chapter 4

Gender as a Social and Cultural Construction

What does it mean to be a woman or a man? It initially begins with where your head is, with your own identity, then internalizing, and reflecting those things that are consistent with that identity, and acting upon the world in ways that are consistent with those identifications . . . Being a woman is pretty much as I thought it would be. (Rachel, quoted in Kessler and McKenna, 1978, pp. 174 and 178)

Introduction

Sex and gender are very important aspects of our personal identity, fundamental to how we perceive both ourselves and others. When a child is born, we want to know immediately if it is a boy or a girl, and the way we react to this information is based on a whole set of social and cultural assumptions about that individual's gendered future. Although gender is usually ascribed to babies on the basis of perceived anatomical distinctions, our assumptions about the child's future are more to do with social and cultural values than with the direct consequences of such bodily features; we assume, however, that these cultural differences will follow fairly automatically from the physical ones. In this chapter I am going to suggest that this assumption is in itself culturally produced, and that the complex of sex, gender identity and gender role naturalizes socially produced power asymmetries in such a way as to give spurious 'scientific' support to prevailing gender inequalities in Western society.

For the sake of clarity, I want to start by distinguishing a number of terms, and explaining how I intend to use them. The meanings of these terms are all more or less a matter of dispute in the literature regarding sex and gender, and can be used in conflicting ways by different authors. Furthermore, some of them are themselves constructed in such a way as to support inequality and will, because of this, be deconstructed later in the chapter. Accordingly, these are only fairly general and approximate definitions, constructed for the purpose of making distinctions between the different kinds of thing I am going to be talking about.

By *sex* I refer to matters of biology. Although, as I shall explain later, even how we understand matters of biology is culturally constructed, a person's sex is usually taken to be a matter of biological fact. It is often seen as a given which is prior to the construction of an individual's gender, a site upon which particular gender characteristics are superimposed (Nicholson, 1994).

Gender assignment (Kessler and McKenna, 1978) is usually a once-and-for-all event based on physical characteristics at birth. A newborn baby is assigned a gender after physical examination. Usually, but not always, this assignment is consonant with (some definition of) biological sex.

Gender identity refers to a person's own feelings about whether they are male, female, both or neither. Such an identity may be different to their assigned gender. It is the gender they attribute to themselves, and is usually established by age 3. The only way to establish someone's gender identity is to ask them; gender identity is a private experience (Kessler and McKenna, 1978; Money and Ehrhardt, 1972).

Finally, gender role refers to a set of behavioural prescriptions or proscriptions for individuals who have a particular assigned gender. These will vary between cultures (Kessler and McKenna, 1978; Nicholson, 1994; Money and Ehrhardt, 1972; Whitehead, 1981). In order to distinguish matters of gender role from those of gender assignment, gender identity and biological sex, I shall generally talk of masculinity and femininity in this context.

Much of what we in Western society take for granted as 'natural' as regards sex and gender is not only socially constructed but conceived of in a way that is fundamentally androcentric, that is, seen from the point of view of and prioritizing the male gender. This androcentrism is also bound up with a dualistic view of both sex and gender in which a person is regarded as either male or female, or, because of this androcentric bias, as male or not-male, male or Other. Bem (1993) refers to this as 'gender polarization', and argues that social life is organized around a dualistic male/female distinction. This distinction provides mutually exclusive ways of being male or female; persons or behaviour that do not conform to these (for example someone assigned at birth as male but who subsequently develops a female gender identity) are regarded as problematic.

Much of the discussion in this chapter is going to focus on such 'problem cases' which do not conform to our naturalized ideas of what constitutes maleness and femaleness, masculinity and femininity. Such cases are interesting because they highlight certain features of our taken for granted assumptions and call their presumed naturalness into question (Kessler and McKenna, 1978). 'Problem' cases also highlight the importance (and contingency) of what Kessler and McKenna call 'gender attribution', that is, the decisions we make about other people's gender when we encounter them. They argue that the process of gender attribution is the means whereby we (in the West) construct a world of two genders; we assume that everyone is either male or female and then use the presence or absence of a variety of clues to decide which. Kessler and McKenna argue that we make gender attributions, at least in part, on the basis of superficial clues such as dress, hairstyle and name, independently of what we know about someone's assignment, identity and role. Once an attribution has been made, this structures the way we interpret gender information about an individual. For example, if we make an initial attribution of femaleness to someone who, while having a female gender identity and role, was assigned as a male at birth (a male-to-female transsexual) even the presence of typically 'male' sexual characteristics (such as a deep voice) is unlikely to cause us to reconsider our attribution. Rachel, a male-to-female transsexual whose letters to the authors are presented as an appendix to Kessler and McKenna's book, describes two occasions on which she had to have her name changed on official papers. On the first, the clerk expresses sympathy with her as a woman with a man's name: 'Oh you poor dear. No wonder you want your name changed! Did your mommy really name you Paul?'. When she amends her driving license, the policeman's only comment is, 'Gee. The division of motor vehicles really messed up this license. Wrong name, address and sex' (Kessler and McKenna, 1978, pp. 208–9).

In my discussion, I am going to make an artificial, and dualistic, distinction between sex and gender. This is because I want to challenge the Western cultural assumption that there is a direct causal and necessary connection between the two, and, in particular, between biological sex and the gender role one takes up (Connell, 1995; Nicholson, 1994). In particular, I want to draw attention to the way that the supposedly 'factual' nature of biological sex has underpinned the naturalization of particular gender roles, and, through this, contributed to the Othering of women (Shilling, 1993). However, it should be said at this stage that the sex/gender distinction in itself reflects Western ideological views of the dichotomy between the soul/psyche and the body, a distinction that in itself is androcentric (see Chapter 6). Throughout this discussion it must be remembered that we are embodied as gendered beings, and that bodily forms can be of fundamental importance to an individual's gender identity and to their ability to act in accordance with a prescribed or preferred gender role. Connell (1995) notes, for example, that masculinity in Western society is bound up with bodily performance; because of this, a man whose body is unable to perform in the appropriate way may experience his gender as precarious.

Issues of Biological Sex

It is generally assumed that someone's biological sex is a 'fact' of nature and that it, at least to some extent, determines a person's gender or gender role behaviour. Faced with, for example, gender differences in performance on spatial tasks, some researchers turn automatically to the possibility of differential brain structures for an explanation (Kimura, 1992). Such research, however, is predicated on the assumption that there are only two, clearly distinguishable, biological sexes. Having made this initial distinction, the scientists involved then try to establish differences. While it is the case that we can find 'scientific' criteria that permit us to label the majority of people as either male or female, there remain individuals who do not easily fit such criteria. Who these people are depends on where we draw our biological line.

Before continuing, it will be useful briefly to consider the developmental processes that produce the different bodily characteristics normally regarded as markers of male and female[1]. In reading this, however, it should be borne in mind that the 'truths' of biology, like other cultural artefacts, reflect the androcentric assumptions of Western culture. Fausto-Sterling (1989) argues that this means, among other things, that the embryological development of the female is much less well understood than that of the male, and is often treated simply as resulting from an absence of masculinizing factors.

> I suggest that the pervasiveness of our cultural construction of female as absence, seen in everything from Freudian theory to the non-equivalence of the words male and female in our language (the opposite of male is not female, but non-male) has also insinuated itself into biological theories about male and female development. (p. 328)

Most mammal embryos have one of two chromosomal makeups: two X chromosomes (XX), normally seen as denoting a female, or one X and one Y (XY) normally seen as denoting a male. However, other combinations do exist, although it appears to be essential to have at least one X chromosome for a foetus to be viable (Kessler and McKenna, 1978). Initially, both XX and XY embryos produce unisex gonads which will later develop in either a male or a female direction, and two sets of accessory structures, one of which will develop further and the other of which will degenerate. In female development the gonads become ovaries, and the paramesonephric ducts form the uterus, oviducts and the upper part of the vagina, while the mesonephric ducts degenerate. In the male, the gonads become testes, the mesonephric ducts develop into the epididymal duct and the vas deferens, while the paramesonephric ducts degenerate. The choice of developmental path is determined by the sex chromosomes and by hormones present in the mother's uterus.

In genetically male (XY) embryos, the testes secrete androgens, which stimulate the development of male sex organs. At the same time, the development of female organs is inhibited by another testicular secretion, Mullerian Inhibitory Factor. In genetic (XX) females, an alternative pathway causes the development of female sex and reproductive organs and the suppression of male ones. Fausto-Sterling notes that our knowledge of the two pathways is not equivalent, and that the development of primary female sexual characteristics is generally treated as occurring simply due to the lack of male hormones; female development is posited as taking place in the absence of androgens. She points out that, for example, the influence of maternal hormones is largely ignored, despite evidence that oestrogen can feminize cold-blooded vertebrates such as fish (Fausto-Sterling, 1987, 1989). Even genetically, then, the female is positioned as Other to the central male. In the scientific literature, Fausto-Sterling (1989) points out, 'the all-inclusive "sex-determination" has usually meant *male* sex determination' (p. 327).

In most cases, gender assignment at birth is based on inspection of the baby's genitals. A baby with a penis will be assigned as a boy, one without as a girl. Here, again, femaleness is often treated as absence, in this case the absence of a penis; the presence of a vagina is not necessarily used as a marker of femaleness (Kessler and McKenna, 1978). Money and Ehrhardt (1972), for example, when explaining that genetic males with androgen-insensitivity syndrome (which causes an outwardly female appearance both before and after puberty) are almost always assigned as female, note that:

> Since it is not usual to do a detailed pelvic examination on a newborn girl, it is not discovered that the vagina may be represented only by a dimple. (p. 110)

Because sex is in most cases assigned at birth using evidence from the outward appearance of the genitals, it is possible to consider the relationship between chromosomal sex, assigned sex and the gender identity that subsequently develops. In looking at this, cases in which there is a mismatch between the assigned and chromosomal sex are particularly salient. Androgen-insensitivity syndrome is one such example. A person with this rare condition is genetically male (XY) but unable to react, either pre- or post-natally, to androgens. This means that, although testes develop, the androgens they secrete are unable to bring about the development of other male sexual characteristics, either in utero or at puberty. Such an individual develops outwardly as a female, with a clitoris, vulva, and vaginal opening. Due to the small amount of oestrogen secreted by the testes in both androgen-insensitive and 'normal' genetic males, there is also pubertal feminization of the body corresponding to that which occurs in a 'normal' female. However, because the embryonic Mullerian Inhibitory Factor is still effective, there is no upper part to the vagina and no uterus (Money and Ehrhardt, 1972).

Such children are almost always assigned and reared as females, develop female gender identity and take on feminine gender roles. Indeed, it may only be when menstruation fails to commence as expected that it is realized that there is anything unusual about them. In the literature there are occasional examples of androgen-insensitive individuals being assigned as male due to the presence of testes, despite having a clitoris instead of a penis. Such individuals develop a male gender identity and masculine role, and experience great distress when, at puberty, their bodies become feminized; because of their androgen-insensitivity it remains impossible to masculinize their bodies in the way that is done, for example, for female-to-male transsexuals (Money and Ehrhardt, 1972). Studies of individuals with comparatively rare combinations of the sex chromosomes (XO, XXY, XYY, etc.) also suggest that, whatever the effects in terms of ability to reproduce, functioning of sexual

Gender as a Social and Cultural Construction

organs, and so on, their gender identities develop in accordance with their gender assignment at birth. This also seems to be the case with individuals born with ambiguous genitalia. Money and Ehrhardt's (1972), admittedly fairly small-scale, studies of the development of matched pairs of genetic females born with hermaphrodite genitals because of hormonal abnormalities (in each pair, one was reared male, one female) suggest that gender identity is not determined either by chromosomal sex or by the action of prenatal hormones.

The only time when sex chromosomes alone are used in distinguishing males from females is in deciding who is permitted to compete as a man or a woman in athletics and other sporting competitions (Burton-Nelson, 1994–5). Because of the presumed differences in prowess between men and women, what is at stake here is whether apparently female athletes are 'really' (here constructed as genetically) male. In this case, the scientific testability of genetic status is seen as providing definitive answers to questions of biological sex. It is clear, however, that an assumption of sexual dimorphism underlies such testing, coupled with a belief that sex chromosomes unequivocally determine physical characteristics. Those excluded from competing in women's events may in fact have a variety of chromosomal statuses. Kessler and McKenna (1978) report the case of Eva Klobukowska, who had won several medals at the 1964 Olympics, and who was declared by the International Amateur Athletic Federation in 1967 to be ineligible to compete as a female; it is likely, they suggest, that she had some XO and some XXY cells. Genetic males with androgen-insensitivity syndrome would also be excluded on these criteria, despite the fact that their bodies are able only to exhibit female physical characteristics, and so, from the point of view of the ideas of 'fairness' underlying genetic testing in sport, are paradigmatically female (Burton-Nelson, 1994–5)[2].

The Development of Gendered Identities and Roles

The above account suggests that neither prenatal hormones nor genetic sex have a significant effect on the development of a male or female gender identity. There have been some studies suggesting that prenatal hormones can have an effect on the adoption of masculine or feminine gender roles (Money and Ehrhardt, 1972), but such effects can be explained by other, postnatal, factors (Bem, 1993) and, in any case, are relatively small (Connell, 1995). So why is it that we experience boys and girls as being different from such a very early age? The research suggests that differently assigned children are treated differently by parents and other adults. Evidence for this comes from studies of how parents are observed to treat babies of differently assigned genders.

Evidence from clinicians treating infants born with ambiguous genitalia (i.e. those with unusual combinations of 'female' and 'male' sexual organs or reproductive features), for example, supports the view that the way a child is reared is the key factor in determining gender identity. In such cases it is generally regarded as appropriate practice to settle (sometimes after several months of tests) on a gender assignment to which the outward appearance of the genitalia (which may include a clitoris so enlarged that it looks like a penis, or a penis that resembles a clitoris) can be made to correspond most closely. In general, the child, once this assignment has been accepted by the parents, develops a corresponding gender identity and role (Money and Ehrhardt, 1972; Kessler, 1990), although recent research suggests that, for this to be fully effective, such assignments or reassignments need to take place within the first few months after birth (Diamond and Sigmundson, 1997). In cases where the gonadic sex is ambiguous, the assigned gender may be completely contrary to the chromosomal sex, suggesting that it is the social results of the former, rather than the latter, that influences gender identity and role behaviour.

Of course, the parents of these children may consciously be trying to establish their child's new gender assignment, both for themselves and for others, particularly if this assignment has taken some time to determine. They may, therefore, be more likely than other parents to emphasize the child's gender identity and what would be an 'appropriate' role. These clinical findings, however, are supported by a study carried out by Smith and Lloyd (1978), who looked at how the perceived gender of an infant affected adult-child interactions. Thirty-two mothers of infants between 5 and 10-months-old were asked to play with an unknown, 6-month-old, baby for ten minutes. The babies (both males and females) were presented by their own mothers and given a name that reflected the clothing they were wearing but not necessarily their biological sex. It was found that the mothers interacted with 'boys' and 'girls' differently. From a choice of toys, only 'girls' were first offered a doll. 'Boys' were given more verbal encouragement to crawl, walk or engage in other large-scale physical action than were perceived girls, and gross motor behaviour of the infant was responded to with whole body stimulation more often with perceived boys than perceived girls. Smith and Lloyd suggest that from a very early age children of different assigned genders are given different behavioural messages by parents. A child's gender assignment leads parents and others to modify, from infancy, their behaviour and responses to the child according to its perceived sex; this causes the child's gender role to develop in particular ways. This, of course, elicits gendered responses from parents and others, which further distinguish the life experiences of male and female children.

As they get older, differentiation into stereotypical gender roles is also reinforced and, indeed, policed, by children themselves. Children are aware of gender from quite an early age. Lloyd and Duveen (1992) report that by age 2–3 they can label themselves and identify the gender marking of domestic artefacts. By age 2, they already show gender-marked behavioural preferences and play more with stereotypically gender-appropriate toys, and even before age 3 they interact more with children of their own gender. Martin and Little (1990) have found that the ability to label according to gender precedes and may be a prerequisite for gender-stereotyped preferences regarding toys and peers. This suggests that such choices are used as part of the process of establishing oneself as being of a particular gender. As any Western infant teacher will confirm, children in the early years of schooling have tremendously stereotyped views about gender-appropriate group membership and behaviour (Lloyd and Duveen, 1992; Francis, 1997). Such attitudes reflect the need of developing children to understand who they are in a society in which a dualistic approach to gender underpins everyday experience.

> Children are born into a particular society and become competent, functioning individuals with particular social identities to the extent that they re-construct for themselves the social representations of the significant groups in their society. (Lloyd and Duveen, 1992, p. 27)

Given that, in Western society, male and female are, stereotypically at least, clearly differentiated social groups, children will need to internalize these group distinctions in order to function as social actors (Davies, 1989; Walkerdine, 1989). Furthermore, because there is an asymmetrical power relation embedded in the construction of the two genders, such distinctions are particularly salient for boys. They need to establish themselves as clear members of the powerful cultural group, in an immediate context (the home, the primary school) where the person with day-to-day power over them is usually female (Walkerdine, 1988). In accordance with this, boys have been found to be more stereotyped in their ideas about gender-appropriate behaviour and dress, and more likely to form and enforce single-sex peer groupings; girls are more likely to abandon a social organization and gender marking based on a dualistic opposition (Lloyd and Duveen, 1992; Bem, 1993; Boldt, 1996; Warin, 1995; Lobel and Menshari, 1993). At school, gender exclusivity and stereotypical behaviour are often unwittingly and, in the teeth of teachers' coexisting beliefs about antisexism, reinforced by the child-centred ideology of the infant classroom. A stress on the importance of children's 'natural' development and self-expression leaves unchallenged their policing of themselves and each other (Burman, 1994; Walkerdine and the Girls and Mathematics Unit, 1989). The most conservative group in the classroom is thus allowed to regulate the expression of gender identities (Lloyd and Duveen, 1992). Similar processes and asymmetries are found in adolescence; these will be discussed in Chapter 8.

The Construction of Gender and Gender Roles in Western Society

I have spent so much time and space on the foregoing two sections because it is necessary to be clear that, though non-physical gender differences are observable even in young children, these are mainly due to factors other than biology. This is important because there is a long tradition of using biological explanations as a way of naturalizing social inequality, between races as well as between genders (Bem, 1993). The different life experiences of assigned males and females from birth, can explain even the small differences that have been found in brain structures. Current thinking in neuroscience suggests that neuronal connections are selectively strengthened as a result of experience (Sacks, 1993); differential experience will lead to differences in neural connections. Men and women do experience the world in different ways, both because of their different bodies and because they are differently positioned in society, and these experiences are likely to have an influence on the ways in which their brains function. Even the ways in which people use their bodies will vary historically and culturally; stereotypical gender role behaviour, including that related to bodily forms and functions, is culturally produced rather than innate.

What I want to discuss in the last section of this chapter is what it is that is constructed as gender in Western society, what are the implications of this construction, and how it contributes to the Othering of particular groups, especially women. Although in Western society gender identity is seen as central to an individual's biography (Brittan, 1989), and although to some extent each person develops their own interpretation and enactment of masculinity and femininity (Chodorow, 1995), at the same time gender is a collective phenomenon, an aspect of social relations as well as of personal life (Kessler and McKenna, 1978; Connell, 1994). This means that the meanings and practices of gender will vary according to culture, race, era, etc. (Flax, 1990). The dominant 'gender scripts' in a particular society are manifestations of that society's ways of classifying and thinking about gender; these are rooted in wider cosmological practices and patterns of social privilege and obligation (Whitehead, 1981). What I discuss below applies predominantly to Western society in the late twentieth century; while some of what I say may be true of other eras or cultures, not all of it will be. I am going to focus on three aspects of the way we construct gender: as dimorphic, as involving a power relation, and as incorporating compulsory heterosexuality.

Gender as Dimorphic

Central to our conception of gender is the assumption that there are two and only two genders, and that people develop either a masculine or a feminine gender identity. Davies (1989) puts the position very clearly:

> Far from 'sex' naturally giving rise to gendered practices, it would seem that the possession of a particular set of genitals obliges the possessor to achieve the ways of being that appear to be implicated in the particular set of genitals they happen to have. (p. 237)

A person or behaviour deviating from this prescription is seen as problematic (Bem, 1993), although our interpretation of the 'problem' remains in gender dimorphic terms. Transsexuals, for example, believe themselves to be of one gender, but in the 'wrong' sort of body (i.e. of the 'wrong' biological sex), not to be a member of an intermediate gender.

This dimorphic view of gender, while common to many societies, is not universal (Kessler and McKenna, 1978; Nicholson, 1994). For example, in two isolated villages in the Dominican Republic, a rare enzyme deficiency led, before the recognition and treatment of the condition in the mid-1970s, to some genetically male children, born with ambiguous genitals, being raised as girls. Between the ages of 7 and 12 these children realized, as they became more physically masculine, that they were different from other girls, and gradually came to evolve male gender identities and roles. The researchers studying this group argue that this change is evidence for the influence of androgens on male gender identity and role (Imperato-McGinley et al., 1979). However, the number of affected individuals within a small and isolated area (thirty-eight were identified from twenty-three interrelated families, and some families had more than one affected child) suggests that, within this community, initial gender assignment might well have been seen as more provisional than it is elsewhere, being confirmed only at puberty. Imperato-McGinley et al. (1979) note that affected individuals were described locally as 'machihembra', which translates as 'first woman, then man', which also suggests that dimorphism and constancy were not central to these people's conception of gender.

Many native North American groups had, until the early twentieth century, an institutionalized intermediate gender, berdache, described to observers as 'man-woman', 'part-man, part-woman' or 'not-man, not-woman' (Whitehead, 1981, p. 88)[3]. The berdache was usually a biological and initially assigned male who, as a child or adult, took on women's work, dress and social, including marital, status. S/he was seen as a mixed creature, with less status than a man but more than a woman. Unlike a transsexual, the berdache's anatomy was, in most tribal groups, not seen as a problem for his/her gender identity but to some extent was bound up in that intermediate identity and role (Whitehead, 1981; Wilson, 1996).

Whitehead (1981) argues that the acceptability of the berdache role was largely due to the comparatively small power asymmetry between women and men in the native North American groups in which it took place. Women were skilled craftworkers who were able to keep and use the proceeds of their work and were honoured for their skill. Furthermore, genitals, though used for initial assignment, were comparatively unimportant markers of gender; occupational roles were seen as far more salient. Western society, however, has a long tradition of gender inequality in which androcentrically-viewed biological differences have been used to naturalize social structures (McNay, 1992). Perceived biological dimorphism has been translated into an asymmetrical gender dimorphism which makes the construction of female as Other more likely.

Gender Roles Involve a Power Relation

Gender dimorphism, including biological dimorphism, is constructed for particular ends; power relations between men and women in Western society require an exaggeration of the differences between them (McNay, 1992; Connell, 1987; di Stefano, 1990). Perceived biological differences are translated into mutually-exclusive gender roles in which what is expected of males and females is played out. Those things particular to the masculine role (in Western society, work outside the home, aggressive behaviour) are given power and status; those to the feminine (care of children, 'service' jobs) are not. Generally, it would appear that the status of an occupation or preference is directly related to which gender is usually associated with it. For example, when typewriters were first invented, they were usually operated by the one or two men in an office of female clerks; typing was seen as a skilled occupation with some status. As typewriters became more widespread, more women started using them, until typing became a low-status, almost entirely feminized, occupation.

Because gender-role differences are so intimately bound up with power relations, their construction is asymmetrical in a number of ways. In our everyday gender attributions, it is male rather than female markers that are salient; as in assignment at birth, the sign of femaleness is the absence of male cues. This is even the case for infants born with ambiguous genitalia: Kessler (1990) notes that the key indicator for the assignment of such an individual as male is the presence (or potential presence, after surgery and hormone treatment) of an adequately functioning penis; if this is not considered achievable, the child is reared as female and a vulva and vagina constructed if necessary.

> The guidelines are clear, but they focus on only one physical feature, one that is distinctly imbued with cultural meaning. This becomes especially apparent in the case of an XX infant with normal female reproductive gonads and a perfect penis. Would the size and shape of the penis, in this case, be the deciding factor in assigning the infant 'male', or would the perfect penis be surgically destroyed and female genitals created? . . . researchers concur that parents are likely to want to raise a child with a normal-shaped penis (regardless of size) as 'male', particularly if the scrotal area looks normal and if the parents have no experience with intersexuality . . . This reasoning implies . . . that it is preferable to remove the internal female organs, implant prosthetic testes, and regulate the 'boy's' hormones for his entire life than to overlook or disregard the perfection of the penis. (pp. 18–19)

Kessler and McKenna (1978), in a study in which subjects were presented with a selection of differently ambiguous (i.e. having both penis and breasts, or vagina and broad, hairy chest) clothed and unclothed figures, found that even clothed ambiguous figures were seen as male. They suggest that external stimuli are filtered through androcentric gender attributions, so that even female cues, such as breasts, can be read as male. For example, in the presence of a penis, 96 per cent of respondents said the figure was a male; the presence of a vagina, alongside male secondary sexual characteristics, was ignored by 30 per cent of participants, who made a male attribution.

A further elaboration and exaggeration of physical differences between men and women is in the requirement that masculine power be physically demonstrated in the body. Berger (1972) suggests that a man's presence depends on the promise of power that he embodies. In Western countries, images of ideal masculinity are constructed and promoted most systematically throughout competitive sport (Connell, 1995; 1987). This is taken up by Shilling (1993), who notes that, even though this promise of power may be conveyed through dress and demeanour rather than muscularity,

> If a man's physicality is unable to convey an image of power, he is found to have little presence precisely because the social definition of men as holders of power is not reflected in his embodiment. (p. 113)

A man who does not have the requisite musculature has to perform his masculinity in other ways, for example by taking on stereotypically masculine interests, activities or social roles (Connell, 1995). It is notable that a woman presenting herself as physically powerful takes herself outside the feminine while still being denied the power the muscular male achieves; this can be experienced as a threat to her gender identity (Paechter and Head, 1996a).

The inscription of masculinity and femininity on the body in this way emphasizes the performative nature of gender roles. In seeing gender as performative I am explicitly regarding it as something that is achieved, worked on (Kessler and McKenna, 1978; McNay, 1992), something that is not natural but which provides an illusion of naturalness which is seen as justifying power differentials (Weir, 1994). Kessler and McKenna (1978) note that what transsexuals have to do consciously is no more than what we all do, but unconsciously: everyone is engaged in 'passing', displaying for others the gender we wish to have attributed to us. Butler (1990) writes that:

> That the gendered body is performative suggests that it has no ontological status apart from the various acts which constitute its reality . . . acts and gestures, articulated and enacted desires create the illusion of an interior and organizing gender core. (p. 136)

The political and discursive origin of gender identity, she argues, is displaced onto the illusory psychological 'core'. What this implies is that in order to preserve our sense of gender identity, we as individuals have to perpetuate and regulate our performance of the gender roles seen as 'appropriate' by society. Furthermore, she suggests, the masculine subject's power and autonomy depends on feminine reflection of it. Similarly, Davies

(1989) argues that our current understandings of what it is to be a person require individuals to take themselves up as distinctively male or female. The opposition embedded in these terms is one in which part of the definition of one is dominance over the other. This means that males have much more invested in the policing of the masculine/feminine boundary than do females and the requirement to 'perform' gender therefore becomes very important for males (Mac an Ghaill, 1996). As femaleness may be ascribed in the absence of male cues, to be recognized as male, one has to ensure that one continues to exhibit the marks of maleness, masculine behaviour. Masculine behaviour is thus more narrowly circumscribed than is feminine. As a result, more boys than girls are perceived as 'gender disordered' and there are more sanctions, both legal and social, on male than on female homosexuality (Bem, 1993).

Compulsory Heterosexuality

Boldt (1996) points out that 'normal' femininity and masculinity have neither intelligibility nor power without the contrasting presence of 'abnormality'. In Western society, normality and abnormality are particularly strongly constructed around sexuality and sexual orientation; desire is constituted in heterosexual terms (Butler, 1990). Connell (1987) notes that what constitutes an object of desire is organized by the dichotomy and opposition of feminine and masculine; each is expected to desire the other, and part of the Othering of women is bound up with masculine desire. Young (1994) points out that, as part of the construction of gender, the assumptions and practices of hetero-sexuality themselves define the meaning of bodies; for example, women's bodies are used as objects of exchange between men (Rich, 1980; Young, 1994). Furthermore, sexual practice is organized around heterosexual couple relation-ships in which sexual difference is seen as providing erotic flavour (Connell, 1987). All of this has a number of effects on the construction of masculine and feminine roles and, as a result, gender identities (Holloway, 1984).

One illustration of how compulsory heterosexuality works in practice is in the clinical assessment of transsexuals. In order to be accepted for surgery, a transsexual has to show both psychiatrists and surgeons that s/he 'really' is of the opposite gender to his/her bodily status. This involves, among other things, conforming to stereotypical gender roles; the male-to-female transsexual has to demonstrate femininity as well as female gender identity. Such an identity includes a heterosexual orientation; it does not seem to be considered possible to be a gay or lesbian post-reassignment transsexual (Diamond and Sigmundson, 1997). For example, Kessler and McKenna (1978) note that

> A psychiatrist reports . . . that he helped a patient realize that he was not
> really a male-to-female transsexual because he continued relating sexually

to women. 'So finally . . . I asked him: "What do you want to be, a Lesbian?" And that crystallized the contradiction for him . . .' (p. 118)

The construction of heterosexuality as a necessary part of gender identities and roles is, clearly, a major factor in the oppression of those who do not conform to gendered sexual scripts. Lesbians and gay men can be understood as challenging stereotypical views of gender role; this threatens the power relations naturalized in gender dimorphism by undercutting the supposed facts of gender difference. Both gay men and lesbians present a threat to masculine power (Rich, 1980). The former, in giving up the hetero-sexuality constructed as central to masculinity, blur the boundary between who counts as a man and who does not (Buchbinder, 1994); this boundary is essential to the preserving of gendered power differentials. The latter, by not positioning themselves as objects of the male objectifying gaze, threaten the legitimacy of that gaze. Mac an Ghaill (1996) notes that the policing of girls in school under the gaze of young heterosexual men includes the use of 'lezzie' as an insult aimed at forcing gender conformity.

We can respond to the inclusion of compulsory heterosexuality in the construction of gender identities and roles in a number of ways. Some writers have suggested, for example, that it puts gay men and lesbians outside the male/female dichotomy; Butler (1990) quotes Wittig as suggesting that an alternative to being male or female is to be lesbian. However, as Butler points out, this is to construct a false dichotomy between homosexual and heterosexual identity and practices; structures of heterosexuality remain within gay and lesbian relationships, and vice versa. Furthermore, she notes,

> Lesbianism that defines itself in radical exclusion from heterosexuality deprives itself of the capacity to resignify the very heterosexual constructs by which it is partially and inevitably constituted. As a result, that lesbian strategy would consolidate compulsory heterosexuality in its oppressive forms. (p. 128)

In pointing this out, Butler is saying something very important. If gender is socially constructed, the current dominant manifestation of that construction is open to contestation and challenge. Once we understand that gender differences are not matters of biological imprinting, we can start to challenge society's conception of gender and start to reconceive and reconstruct gender roles in accordance with a more equitable system of power relations.

Summary

This chapter has outlined the ways in which gender is socially constructed in Western society, in particular as being dimorphic, incorporating a power relation and requiring compulsory heterosexuality.

Key Points

- Much of what we take for granted as 'natural' in Western society, as regards sex and gender, is socially constructed and androcentric.
- How we determine an individual's biological sex is also a social and cultural construction, involving, for example, ideas about sexual dimorphism that do not reflect physical or chromosomal 'realities'.
- In the majority of cases, gender identity is related to biological sex, but this is not a necessary relation and, in some cases, the two are unrelated.
- Biological explanations have been used to support prevailing social inequalities by naturalizing gender roles.
- The meanings and practices of gender vary according to culture, race, era, etc.
- Gender has been seen as dimorphic in most cultures of which we have records, as it is in contemporary Western society. However, there have been exceptions to this, which implies that this is not a necessary or essential perception.
- Differences in gender roles involve a power relation in which 'masculine' activities are given higher status than 'feminine' ones; what these activities actually are will vary.
- Gender is performed, in part through the body.
- Because of the power relation inherent in constructed gender differences, masculinity is more precarious, and therefore more defended than femininity; this leads to there being more restricted behavioural possibilities for males than for females.
- Compulsory heterosexuality is an important part of the social construction of gender in Western society.

Question
How important is the cultural assumption of gender dimorphism in the perpetuation of unequal power relations between masculine and feminine gender roles? Would undermining this assumption have a corresponding effect on these power relations?

Further Reading

KESSLER, S. and McKENNA, W. (1978) *Gender: An Ethnomethodological Approach*, New York: John Wiley and Sons, is a classic study of the social construction of gender. It contains as an appendix extracts from letters to the authors from Rachel, a pre-operative transsexual, which are very illuminative of the process of 'performing gender'.

RICH, A. (1980) 'Compulsory heterosexuality and lesbian existence', *Signs*, **5**, 4, pp. 631–60 is another classic, this time looking at the phenomenon of compulsory heterosexuality from a lesbian point of view.

For those interested in early childhood education and gender socialization, LLOYD, B. and DUVEEN, G. (1992) *Gender Identities and Education: The Impact of Starting School*, Hemel Hempstead, Herts: Harvester Press, is worth a read.

CONNELL, R.W. (1987) *Gender and Power*, Cambridge: Polity Press, is an excellent analysis of the relationship between gender and power.

Notes

1 This explanation is based on Fausto-Sterling, A. (1987, 1989).
2 This was successfully challenged by Maria Patino in 1988, who was reinstated after being banned as an androgen-insensitive XY female. However, as Burton-Nelson (1995) points out, most of those banned fake injury and depart quietly rather than expose themselves to the publicity of challenging their exclusion. Burton-Nelson also notes the paradoxical situation in which male-female transvestites, usually chromosomically XY, are excused chromosomal testing on the grounds of equality of opportunity.
3 Wilson (1996) argues that this role persists, but is now available to women as well as men. She rejects the label 'berdache' as colonial, preferring the designation 'two-spirit people'. While acknowledging its colonial inheritance, I have retained the former term partly because it is the one found in the anthropological literature, and partly because Wilson seems to see gay/lesbian orientation as central to two-spiritedness, which does not accord with my reading of the anthropological accounts.

Chapter 5

Reconceptualizing Gender Issues in Education

Power in the substantive sense, '*le pouvoir*', doesn't exist. What I mean is this. The idea that there is either located at — or emanating from — a given point something which is a 'power' seems to me to be based on a misguided analysis, one which at all events fails to account for a considerable number of phenomena. In reality power means relations, a more-or-less organised, hierarchical, coordinated cluster of relations . . . If one tries to erect a theory of power one will always be obliged to view it as emerging at a given place and time and hence to deduce it, to reconstruct its genesis. But if power is in reality an open, more-or-less coordinated (in the event, no doubt, ill-coordinated) cluster of relations, then the only problem is to provide oneself with a grid of analysis, which makes possible an analytic of relations of power. (Foucault, 1980, pp. 198–9)

Introduction

So far in this book we have discussed three main areas. First, I looked at the position of the female as Other in Western society, and outlined how this applied to education. I then went on to describe in some detail the ways in which this Otherness is manifested in the school setting, concentrating in particular on the differential experiences of males and females in the classroom, subject takeup in secondary schools, issues of assessment and achievement and deficit models as they are applied to girls and young women in schools. Third, I looked at the ways in which gender is socially and culturally constructed in Western society, laying particular stress on the contingency of such constructions. In this chapter I want to move on and start to consider whether we have to continue with the gender regimes that prevail in our schooling systems. I shall argue that such regimes are always and by their very nature open to challenge, and that the key to such challenge is an understanding of how they operate.

The gender regime currently encountered by girls in schools and in wider Western society is hegemonic; it is so deeply embedded in social and cultural forms that most of the time it feels natural and inevitable. For example, when we see primary school girls acting as helpers, or those in secondary school avoiding physical education, it is easy to interpret that behaviour as something girls simply do. Once we call this assumption of naturalness into question, however, we can come to understand that, although constrained to certain behaviours by a number of overlapping social forces, girls do not have to act in this way. We can also challenge the ways particular behaviours are interpreted and judged. The key to both these forms of resistance is understanding. In particular, we have to find ways of coming to a clearer perception of what constitutes the relationship between power and gender, both in the school and in the wider social context.

Power/Gender

In Chapter 4 I argued that gender is constructed in such a way as to involve or include an unequal power relation, such that, while there are of course differences within genders, it is (mainly) males who have access to, enact and embody power. We have now to look in more detail at this relationship between gender and power. My own view of power follows that of Foucault (1977, 1978, 1979, 1980, 1982, 1988), but with a greater emphasis on the gender/power relation, which is given fairly low priority in his writing. According to this account, power and its manifestations are not single monolithic entities but are multiple. Power is not held solely by one individual or group, but is distributed in complex ways throughout a social world. It is thus understood as:

> the moving substrate of force relations which, by virtue of their inequality, constantly engender states of power, but the latter are always local and unstable. The omnipresence of power: not because it has the privilege of consolidating every thing under its invincible unity, but because it is produced from one moment to the next, at every point, or rather in every relation from one point to another. Power is everywhere; not because it embraces everything, but because it comes from everywhere. (Foucault, 1978, p. 93)

What this means is that power does not emanate from one source and cannot be held in any permanent way by individuals. It is inscribed in our social forms, in our ways of being and in the spaces we inhabit. It means that we cannot specify that one person or institution has and holds power, by virtue of their position or through moral or physical force (Foucault, 1980). Power is everywhere, it is in our institutions and our relationships, in the ways we move and the language we use.

> Power is not something that is acquired, seized, or shared, something that one holds on to or allows to slip away; power is exercised from innumerable points, in the interplay of nonegalitarian and mobile relations. (Foucault, 1978, p. 94)

Power is not something that is wielded solely by the state or by a dominant social group; it is something that can be used (though not equally) by all. Power is conceived of as coming from below; instead of emanating from the centralized power of state or sovereign, it is exercised in micro-situations, in relations between individuals. Foucault sees power as beginning in small interactions and spreading to the wider social arena, rather than the other way round, and he argues that it is to the interplay of these small interactions that we must direct our study. Such a conception of power has effects both on how we analyse its operation and on how we resist it. By focusing on the exercise of power, Foucault is laying stress on the mechanisms through which this exercise takes place, rather than on who, in particular, is wielding power at any one time.

> And I don't believe that the question of 'who exercises power?' can be resolved unless that other question, 'how does it happen?' is resolved at the same time. Of course we have to show who those in charge are . . . But this is not the important issue, for we know perfectly well that even if we reach the point of designating exactly all those people, all those 'decision makers', we will still not really know why and how the decision was made, how it came to be accepted by everybody, and how it is that it hurts a particular category of person, etc. (Foucault, 1988, pp. 103–4)

This way of looking at power, as residing in relations rather than in persons or institutions, brings with it a complementary view of resistance, as ever-present, inseparable from the operation of power. Because power relationships are strictly relational, they operate in a constant dialectic with resistance.

> Their existence depends on a multiplicity of points of resistance: these play the role of adversary, target, support, or handle in power relations. These points of resistance are present everywhere in the power network. Hence there is no single locus of great Refusal, no soul of Revolt, source of all rebellions, or pure law of the revolutionary. Instead there is a plurality of resistances, each of them a special case. (Foucault, 1978, pp. 95–6)

This means that, while power is now seen as being everywhere, so is resistance; because power relations are enacted through micro-situations, resistance is also possible at the micro level. There are innumerable, local points at which the matrix of power can be challenged and undermined. Multiple micro-powers, with correspondingly multiple micro-resistances, are therefore set against each other in an intricately woven fabric of interaction. They interrelate in ways that are often ignored in traditional analyses of power relations, which tend to concentrate solely on the acquisition and uses of positional power (Paechter and Head, 1996b), ignoring both resistance and the ways in which power is both invested in persons and inscribed in physical and social forms.

In the school context, for example, power relations can be mapped directly onto the building in terms of both space and time (Hoskin, 1990):

teachers have access to spaces to which students have not, some subjects have more favourable accommodation than others, and some teachers or groups of teachers are able to take up more time on the timetable and space in the staffroom. In some cases, the inscription of power into school spaces is very explicit. Foucault (1978, 1980) notes the ways in which, in the eighteenth century, school buildings in themselves formed apparatuses for the regulation and control of children's sexuality.

> The space for classes, the shape of the tables, the planning of the recreation lessons, the distributions of the dormitories (with or without partitions, with or without curtains), the rules for monitoring bedtime and sleep periods — all this referred, in the most prolix manner, to the sexuality of the children. (Foucault, 1978, p. 28)

More mundanely, the gaps commonly found at the tops and bottoms of school lavatory cubicles similarly permit the more institutionally powerful to observe, and, potentially, prevent occasions when more than one student is present in a space explicitly designed for individual use. At the same time, the supposed privacy of these spaces is an inhibitory force on teachers' intervention, allowing them also to operate as sites for resistance.

Power relations in schools, as in wider society, are often gendered, but different forms of power can be gendered in different ways. Among teachers, for example, men are more likely than women to hold positions of structural power, as headteachers or heads of department. Women, on the other hand, may be able to resist this by using interpersonal alliances to build networks of group power which can make it difficult or impossible for those in structurally powerful roles to take full advantage of their position (Paechter and Head, 1995, 1996b). Similarly, boys' domination of classroom space does not go unchallenged. It has to be continually fought for, with stereotypical models of masculinity and femininity invoked in support of this appropriation of resources; these models are themselves also contested and resisted by both genders. Even though there is a tendency in Western society for masculinity and the assumption of power to go hand in hand, this assumption remains fragile and contested, depending, as we have seen, on perpetuating a distinction between male as Subject and female as Other that itself is subject to constant challenge.

Gender, Power, Pedagogy and the Learning Child

The multiple forms and all-pervasiveness of power mean that its operation is often hidden. In particular, it can form a negative side to what may on the surface appear to be positive features. The welfare state, for example, has as its darker aspect a greatly increased surveillance of individuals; police, social workers and other professionals are employed specifically to look out for and investigate 'abnormal' practices (Foucault, 1982). While health visitors, for example, have as a major function the support of families with young children, they also have an important role in 'child protection', the recognition and investigation of families whose structures or behaviours do not conform to social or moral norms. In order to uncover the hidden power relations within such overtly benign practices, we need to deconstruct the discourses by which they are framed. An example of this which is particularly relevant to the power/gender relation is that of the inscription of particular inter- pretations of developmental psychology into the practices of early childhood education.

The practices underpinning welfare provision, in which all adults and children are subject to surveillance in order to ensure the protection of the few, operate through a 'normalizing gaze'. By this I mean that the individual under scrutiny is constantly compared to an image of the 'normal', based on observations of both 'normal' and 'abnormal' examples, and is further examined or investigated if found wanting. The means by which such norms are both established and then applied to others is the supposedly dispassionate, non-interfering, observing gaze.

> The observing gaze refrains from intervening: it is silent and gestureless. Observation leaves things as they are; there is nothing hidden to it in what is given. (Foucault, 1963, p. 107)

This gaze, in which the child's behaviour is observed but not overtly influenced, forms a fundamental underpinning of developmental psychology as it has been understood since the nineteenth century. Based on an assump- tion of constant and steady progress, developmental theories use studies of 'normal' children in order to establish accounts of expected changes in behaviour and understanding, against which other children can be measured and judged (Morss, 1996). Although most of these theories have been developed from limited populations, often white and male, they are expected to apply to all. Those who do not follow the appropriate path are treated as problems, not for the theory, but for themselves and/or society; their trajectories are seen as pathological. Furthermore, the methods and mores of child development research have been translated into prescriptions for education that are seen to apply to both parent and teacher. The child is treated as an object to be studied, not just so that developmental 'norms' can be established, but also to enable the caring parent or teacher to attune their responses to the individual. Although originally it was believed that mothers were incapable of sufficient detachment to carry out the 'scientific' observation of child study (Burman, 1994), the move from developmental psychology as scientific discovery to its use as a basis for pedagogic prescription has positioned both mothers and (usually female) teachers of young children as having constantly to observe in order to be able to respond appropriately to the individual child. This goes hand in hand with an ideology of early childhood education, emerging in the late nineteenth century with the introduction of women into teaching, in which female teachers are expected to be loving and responsive in a manner that parallels ideologies of the 'good mother' (Burman, 1994; Walkerdine, 1984).

In this approach to the education of children, which has its roots in a variety of theories of developmental psychology, the child's development is seen as 'natural'. The mother/teacher's role is to foster, or at least not to hinder it; she should not overtly teach. The focus is on the child, rather than on what is to be learned; the mother/teacher is expected to follow the child's direction, without having specific or overt learning goals. Burman (1994) suggests that

> Central tenets of the child-centred approach are indicated by five key terms: readiness, choice, needs, play and discovery. 'Readiness' means that the child must be ready to learn, with learning concerned with social and emotional, as well as cognitive, development. 'Choice' highlights how learning should be directed towards the individual interests of the child, and that the child should dictate the timing and content of the learning process. In terms of 'needs', children are seen to have fundamental needs, the failure to meet which gives rise to later (both individual and social) problems . . . The focus on 'play' suggests that learning should be voluntary, enjoyable, self-directed, non-goal oriented, functional for emotional well-being and that the general opposition between work and play should be broken down. The promotion of autonomy was seen as central to fostering curiosity, confidence and competence, in which play functioned as the guarantor of freedom and independence. Finally, the role of 'discovery' highlights that learning takes place through individual, personal experience. (pp. 164–5)

Fostering child-centred learning requires constant self-surveillance on the part of the mother/teacher, with concomitant guilt if the injunction, to allow 'natural' development to proceed at the child's own pace, is transgressed (Walkerdine, 1984, 1989). At the same time, by treating development as a 'natural' progression, it devalues and ignores the hard work and creative thought of teaching and parenting (Morss, 1996). Meanwhile, though the mother/teacher's constant and vigilant presence and facilitation are required, she is at the same time seen as a potential threat to that development, in constant danger of inhibiting the child's discovery of the world.

Furthermore, not only is the parent/teacher positioned as a nurturant, ever-attentive female, the active learning child is, in this model, seen as male. The discourse of child development as 'natural', within a context of the mother as a nurturer and facilitator, constructs a 'couple' modelled on the conventional heterosexual dyad of the servicing female dancing attendance on the active male; Burman (1995) points out that in the childcare manuals of the 1940s and 1950s mother and child were even referred to as a 'couple'. The discourse of development also privileges culturally masculine qualities; the developmental trajectory is expected to move from (feminine) attachment to (masculine) detachment (see Chapter 6), while the theoretical framework upon which Piagetian and related developmental theories are based, regards masculine and Western forms of reasoning as the most primary intellectual goals (Burman, 1994). The combination of these two features, that development is both natural and takes place along a trajectory modelled on features of white middle-class male society (Walkerdine, 1993), positions female children very definitely as Other within this discourse. Where they feature at all, it is as anomalies.

The discourse of the observing, nurturing mother/teacher figure sensitively supporting the development of the active, exploratory developing male child exerts a strong disciplinary force over both parties. Burman notes that when this discourse is inserted into the practices of early childhood education it can put teachers into a double-bind in which anything they do is likely to be wrong (Walkerdine, 1984).

> A teacher attempting to conform to these precepts encounters an untenable conflict between the mandate for non-interference to promote independence, and her institutional position as responsible for children's learning. How can she oversee the individual development of a class of thirty children? Various studies of both accounts of, and implementation of, 'progressive' education . . . have highlighted how teachers position themselves as both responsible for, but helpless in, moulding children's development. (Burman, 1994, pp. 165–6)

At the same time, the accompanying discourse of development as 'natural' and achieved through enjoyable, 'discovery' activities both blurs the distinction between work and play (by classifying school activities as 'play') while simultaneously counterposing the two, positioning the former as an 'inappropriate' form of learning. For the exploring, child-as-scientist, 'discovering' knowledge, all learning has to come through play, with the result that

> It follows that *work*, as constituted as an opposite of *play*, can be recognized as a difference, as everything which does not signify play. It is also recognised as a danger-point, a point to be avoided. It is pathologized. It is learning by the wrong means. It is not 'natural' to 'the child'. If any child is observed 'doing work' this is likely to be understood as a problem. (Walkerdine, 1988, p. 207)

This counterposition between 'work' as pathological and 'play' as a natural and essential part of developmental learning, has direct effects on the ways in which different children are positioned within classrooms. In school, and in many homes, there is an overt message to children that to work hard is good; there is a constant and repeated injunction to 'get on' and 'not muck about'. Children are praised for concentration, for neatness, for being helpful (Walkerdine, 1989)[1]. At the same time, the discourse of work as pathological means that success resulting from this hard work is judged as inferior to that which is based on 'natural ability' or 'flair'. In particular, those who challenge the teachers' ideas (something discouraged by the discourse of getting on with one's work) are seen as more able. Walden and Walkerdine (1985), for example, document the ways in which hard-working girls' performance at mathematics is perceived as stemming not from 'real understanding' (good) but from 'rote learning' (bad). This is crucially important in terms of access to life chances; in the school they studied girls were entered for lower-level 16+ mathematics examinations than boys who had the same or lower scores in 'mock' examinations. Gipps and Murphy (1994) found similar discrepancies in national examination entry statistics. While girls respond to one set of classroom messages, their success is judged against other standards running counter to these. Given that, particularly in secondary schools, there is also a stigma attached to being a resistant, assertive girl (see Chapter 3) it is not surprising that the message many girls pick up and respond to is that of good behaviour and rule-following. They are then penalized for displaying the very behaviours they have been encouraged to adopt.

Conclusion

The deconstruction of the discourses of child development and child-centred pedagogy is only one example of the ways in which we can undercut and challenge hegemonic networks of power. While it is undeniable that child-centred pedagogy has produced friendlier and more exciting classrooms, it does have a darker side, of which we need to be aware. It is this understanding of the alternate aspect to overtly beneficent structures which allows us to perceive the ways in which they themselves embody and promote particular configurations of power. This perception makes active resistance more possible.

When thinking about girls and women in relation to education, there has been a longstanding tendency to focus on their failures, their lack of fit with the prevailing orthodoxies regarding what counts as high-status knowledge, what is regarded as 'real' learning. It is important, however, to realize that it may not be the girls who are lacking, but the model. Because education has been structured around a dominant male Subject, it should be no surprise that those who are Othered in society are also Othered with respect to the education system.

The implications of this are multifarious. The Othering of girls and young women, particularly those who are black or working-class, still prevents them from being as educationally successful as males, particularly those from white middle-class backgrounds[2]. Furthermore, it pathologizes any lack of fit between themselves and the system, locating it in the individual, while leaving the educational discourse unchallenged. Within schools, girls and young women are subject to a number of gender regimes which limit their educational and social progress, restrict their freedom of movement and expression, and treat as problematic even their conformity to the overt demands of the school. These regimes are indeed powerful. However, if, as I suggested earlier, we regard them as being composed of a constantly changing network of micro-powers, we may, through an analytic understanding of their modes of operation, set in motion appropriate and finely tuned micro-resistances.

The remainder of this book is intended as one move towards that goal. The next three chapters examine in detail three different aspects of the gender/power regimes in schools, focusing on the Othering of particular subordinated groups and discourses. In Chapter 6 I consider the dominance of reason in Western thought, focusing in particular on the ways in which particular, rationalist, forms of ethical thought have come to dominate both moral philosophy and models of moral development. I argue that we need to revalue alternative, particularly female, voices in the context of moral thought and that we need to challenge the hegemonic dominance of reason in Western moral and philosophical thinking. Next, I consider the Others of the school curriculum, looking at the ways in which particular school subjects are dominant and subordinated, and at the relationship between the gendering of curriculum areas and their position within intellectual hierarchies. In Chapter 8 I then move on to consider three groups who inhabit subordinated masculinities and femininities within the school context: those males who do not conform to dominant modes of masculinity, 'sporty' girls, and lesbian and gay students and teachers. Finally, in Chapter 9, using these examples as a background, I suggest some components of a 'toolkit' of strategies for investigating and acting upon issues of Othering in the school context.

Summary

In this chapter I have moved from the initial discussion of female Otherness and how it is manifested in schools, to considering the power/gender relationship in more detail. Using the work of Foucault, I have outlined a conception of power as multiple, operating at the micro level, with corresponding micro-resistances. I then looked at the discourses of child-centred development and pedagogy as examples of the operation of power/gender relations through a seemingly benign discourse. This forms a bridge to the remainder of the book, in which I consider in detail specific instances of the operation of the Othering of particular subordinated groups, before suggesting a number of strategies for further micro-investigation.

Key Points

- Power is not monolithic but multiple and distributed throughout a social world. It is invested in persons and inscribed in physical and social forms.

- Power relations are often gendered.
- Many practices of the welfare state, including that of the overseeing of child development, operate through a 'normalizing gaze'.
- One example of this is the discourse of child development, which has been extremely influential on the pedagogy of the primary classroom in particular. In this discourse, the active, exploratory child is male, the nurturing facilitator female. This positions girls as Other.
- The child-centred approach to pedagogy has a discourse in which 'work' is counterposed to play and pathologized. At the same time, there is an overt message that children should work in school. Girls who take this message on board have their achievements, seen as resulting from 'hard work', rated lower than those of boys, whose success is often attributed to 'natural ability'. This can have important effects on their life chances.

Question

In this chapter, I have used the example of the discourse of early child development to illustrate the workings of the normalizing gaze. In what other contexts does such a gaze operate and what are the power relations contained in it?

Further Reading

The two most accessible of Foucault's works concerning power are: FOUCAULT, M. (1977) *Discipline and Punish: The Birth of the Prison*, London: Penguin, and FOUCAULT, M. (1978) *The History of Sexuality, Volume 1*, London: Penguin. A good collection of articles applying his work specifically to education is: BALL, S.J. (ed.) (1990) *Foucault and Education: Disciplines and Knowledge*, London: Routledge.

For a good text on the deconstruction of developmental psychology, BURMAN, E. (1994) *Deconstructing Developmental Psychology*, London: Routledge, is well worth a read.

Notes

1   Walkerdine (1989) suggests that this message, because it runs in con-traposition to the discourse of child-centred learning, would have by necessity to be covert. My own, feeling is, however, that both messages are operating simultaneously and overtly, as instantiated by the distinction many teachers make between 'working' noise and 'messing about' noise.
2   It should be noted, however, that black girls are generally more successful than their male counterparts (Mirza, 1992).

Chapter 6

Revaluing Female Voices

Whereof one cannot speak, thereof one must be silent. (Wittgenstein, 1922, p. 189)

Challenging the Mastery of Reason

Perhaps, too, we should abandon a whole tradition that allows us to imagine that knowledge can exist only where the power relations are suspended and that knowledge can develop only outside its injunctions, its demands and its interests. Perhaps we should abandon the belief that power makes mad and that, by the same token, the renunciation of power is one of the conditions of knowledge. (Foucault, 1977, p. 27)

In Chapter 2 I introduced the idea of the Other by talking about the way that Western thought has been structured by a series of dichotomies, in which male has been placed on the positive side and the female Other on the negative. In this chapter I want to focus on a particular aspect of this process, looking at the hegemony of reason and rational thought, recent challenges to this, and the implications for educational practice both of the dominance of reason and of the alternatives to it.

One of the difficulties in discussing what Walkerdine (1988) refers to as the 'mastery of reason' is its very hegemony. We are steeped in a tradition in which to be human is to be rational (Gatens, 1991), in which decontextualized knowledge is seen as the most important, the most powerful, and where a particular image of the nature of knowledge constrains even what can be said about it. As Foucault (1988) suggests:

It is not enough to say that science is a set of procedures by which propositions may be falsified, errors demonstrated, myths demystified, etc. Science also exercises power: it is, literally, a power that forces you to say certain things, if you are not to be disqualified, not only as being wrong, but, more seriously than that, as being a charlatan. (p. 107)

You are likely to find this chapter, particularly the opening sections, difficult to read. It is also difficult to write. The terms we have for the alternatives to 'rational' — 'non-rational', 'emotional', 'contextualized' — carry within them a power relation which positions them negatively with regard to reason itself. The power relation is contained within the words, it affects us almost without us noticing; to write against reason seems almost to be an absurdity. I shall attempt to show that this challenge is not absurd at all, and that we even have the language to make it.

I shall start by considering the ways in which power becomes inscribed in practices that value decontextualized knowledge over that which is situated in everyday practices. Ironically, the power of such knowledge partly arises from the illusion that it is in these circumstances that 'the power relations are suspended' (Foucault, 1977); it is assumed that by disconnecting thought from its context we are able to arrive at pure and absolute truths, separate from power relations. This ignores the fundamental association between power and knowledge, in which each is inscribed in the other. The power relations may be obscured, they may be indirectly realized, but they are still there.

The power of reason is a particularly important illustration of this. Rational thought is an attempt to decouple judgments of various kinds from the particular contexts in which they might be made (Smith, 1990). Moral reason, for example, attempts to come to decisions which would have universal applicability; these take the form of 'moral rules' such as 'it is always wrong to take a human life'. It is assumed that the power relations between actual people obscure moral thinking, so such judgments have to be made in the abstract, with moral agents attempting to think as if they were not actors in the situation. Scientific reasoning makes similar attempts to formulate universal laws by suspending the realities of the actual world; scientific principles are formulated to apply in the ideal conditions of frictionless surfaces and pure substances rather than in the polluted, less than perfectly smooth conditions of the laboratory, the engineering workshop, or the world in general.

The paradigmatic case of decontextualized knowledge is that of pure mathematics, and it is here that we can see most clearly the relationship between power and reason. This relationship is close and complex, operating partly through reason itself and partly through our belief in its power. Walkerdine (1988) argues that the decontextualized nature of mathematics holds out 'the dream of a possibility of perfect control in a perfectly rational and ordered universe' (p. 187). Mathematics provides a fantasy of power and control which, although at least on one level chimerical, is part of a discourse in which those seen as having 'mastery' of it are given a real (in the sense of exercisable) power, arising from its possession, rather than from the knowledge directly. Walkerdine stresses the importance of this

> fantasy of a discourse and practice in which the world becomes what is wanted: regular, ordered, controllable. The imposition of this discourse onto the world therefore renders to the mathematician, scientist, psychologist, linguist or whatever an incredibly powerful position. For s/he produces statements which are taken to be true. The result of a fantasy is lived as a fact. (p. 188)

Although this power to control the world is in itself largely illusory, the general belief in the omnipotence of reason and 'objective' truth gives legitimation to the result, which is that those claiming such knowledge are given the power anyway (Connell, 1995; Massey, 1995). Walkerdine (1988) thus argues that

> the modern order is founded upon a rational, scientific, and calculating form of government, a government which claims to describe and control nature, according to natural laws. (p. 211)

Walkerdine suggests that the straightforward link between knowledge and power, the belief that pure, decontextualized knowledge brings power over an ultimately comprehensible universe, is itself a fantasy. Nevertheless, we explicitly open up routes to power within the wider society, through our belief in the knowledge-related power we suppose to be already held by those who have attained the 'mastery of reason' that comes with 'real understanding' of mathematical and scientific laws, by giving them preferential access to higher level certification (see Chapter 3). Furthermore, Walkerdine (1989) argues, femininity is constructed in opposition to a stereotypical masculine rationality to such an extent that femininity is equated with poor mathematical performance, even when the girl or woman under consideration is performing well. Distinctions between 'real understanding' and 'rote learning' are also apparent in the academic/practical divide that lies behind the low status of traditional technology education; the ability to build and maintain working machines is considered to be of lesser value than the understanding of the scientific principles according to which such machines operate. Thus, the fantasy of power and control vested in the understanding of the 'truths' of mathematics and science is translated into actual power within the wider social system.

This power is achieved, however, at a cost. Operating as a rational subject requires, because of the decontextualization involved, sidelining one's contextualized and embodied personhood. It involves a depersonalization, which, while pleasurable because of the illusion of mastery that it brings, is also painful, a denial of the self (Walkerdine, 1988). In particular, it requires a denial of human connectedness. This denial, as we shall see later in this chapter, is particularly problematic for women. At the same time, because the operation of an 'objective' rationality requires the suspension of located subjectivity, it produces a 'degendered' subject. This, because of its association with reason and the transcendence of the body, turns out to be constructed as male.

Reason and the Discourse of Empowerment

I want now to go on and explore in more detail some of the consequences of the relationship between power and reason, through an examination of

the discourse of 'empowerment'. This discourse has been particularly influential in emancipatory Western educational theory in recent years. However,
the centrality of reason to its conception and methodology again leads to
problems for groups, including females, constructed as Other by a supposedly
liberating discourse.

There are a number of overlapping definitions of 'empowerment'
currently to be found in the literature (Lightfoot, 1986). These can broadly
be categorized into two groups, one focused around the personal (for
example, Rogers (1983)) and one around the political and, in particular, the
stances of critical theory (for example, Giroux (1988c)). I shall be concentrating my critique on the latter, in which empowerment is used to mean

> analysing ideas about the causes of powerlessness, recognizing systemic
> oppressive forces, and acting both individually and collectively to change
> the conditions of our lives. (Lather, 1991, pp. 3–4)

While it is generally stressed that empowerment is something that,
ultimately, one has to do for oneself (Lather, 1991), a major concern in the
literature has been to establish how teachers and students can work together
towards their mutual empowerment within the essentially hegemonic framework of the educational institution (Giroux, 1988a; McLeod et al., 1993).
Much of this discussion centres around the ways in which the prevailing
relationship between power and knowledge permits and includes some
knowledges while silencing others. Attempts to interrogate and subvert this
order concern themselves with ways in which students' knowledge can be
given status within the classroom and with ways in which teachers and
students together can work to produce knowledge for themselves. Central
to this is the concept of 'voice' (Giroux, 1988a, b, c; Freire, 1972; Jipson
et al., 1995), which

> represents the unique instances of self-expression through which students
> affirm their own class, cultural, racial and gender identities. A student's voice
> is necessarily shaped by personal history and distinctive lived engagement
> with the surrounding culture. The category of voice, then, refers to the means
> at our disposal — the discourses available to use — to make ourselves
> understood and listened to, and to define ourselves as active participants in
> the outside world. (Giroux, 1988c, p. 199)

An important feature of the life of educational institutions, Giroux argues,
is the way that some voices, in particular those of teachers and of white
middle-class males, are given more legitimation than others (Giroux, 1988c).
He argues that it is therefore essential that those who would wish to develop
an empowering pedagogy give space to those voices that would otherwise
remain silenced (Fitzclarence and Giroux, 1984). Such a concept seems at
first sight to be useful in 'negotiating between the directiveness of dominant
educational relationships and the political commitment to make students

[handwritten: voice - allowing students to have / develop their own]

[handwritten in left margin: we should head alternative voices]

autonomous of those relationships' (Ellsworth, 1989, p. 309). In other words, the idea of 'voice' may be important in helping students to move beyond traditional relationships between teacher and taught, in which the teacher is the knowing Subject and the student the ignorant Other. However, even if we ignore the asymmetry of the underlying assumption of empowerment pedagogy, that it is the teacher who leads the empowerment of the students (McLeod et al., 1993), the processes by which such a pedagogy is expected to operate themselves act to exclude and silence certain voices. They do this by privileging the discourse of reason over alternative, positional discourses, and through an unstated assumption that it is possible to make the class or seminar room into a safe space in which discourses of domination and oppression are sufficiently neutralized to allow for dispassionate examination. Although students are expected to 'give voice' to the particulars of their experience, they are then expected to discuss the issues raised as if the power imbalances they articulate were not present in the classroom. In other words, there is an attempt to suspend power relations, while those very power relations are themselves discussed and dissected. Ellsworth (1989) notes that, despite the stress on the importance of the individual voice, the underlying assumptions of critical pedagogy are rationalist, giving the critical educator only one possible role:

> These rationalist assumptions have led to the following goals: the teaching of analytic and critical skills for judging the truth and merit of propositions, and the interrogation and selective appropriation of potentially transformative moments in the dominant culture. As long as educators define pedagogy against oppressive formations in these ways the role of the critical pedagogue will be to guarantee that the foundation for classroom interaction is reason. In other words, the critical pedagogue is one who enforces the rules of reason in the classroom. (pp. 303–4)

The assumption that reason will neutralize the power imbalances between different groups of students in the interests of the empowerment of all is allowed to remain unchallenged in the writings of critical theorists in part because they tend to make suggestions as to how critical educators should act in the classroom without examining the effects of these proposed practices in the context of real classrooms (Ellsworth, 1989). For example, Giroux (1988c) discusses the 'classic example' of the feminist teacher faced with sexist behaviour from her male students. She reacts by providing feminist curriculum materials, which the students treat with 'scorn and resistance' (p. 164). So far, so likely. But Giroux goes on to argue that:

> Rather than give any attention to how the students produce meaning, the feminist teacher falsely assumes the self-evident nature of the political and ideological correctness of her position. In doing so, she assumes an authoritative discourse which disallows the possibility for the students to 'tell' their own stories, and to present and then question the experiences they bring

into play. Then, by denying students the opportunity to question and investigate the ideology of sexism as a problematic experience, the teacher not
only undermines the voices of these students, but she displays what in their
eyes is just another example of institutional/middle class authority telling
them what to think. (p. 164)

This seems fine until you start to think about how Giroux's preferred
strategy would work in an actual classroom. What Giroux seems to be
suggesting here is that the teacher should encourage the students to articulate
their sexist views, so that they can be put under rational scrutiny by the
students themselves, with the (presumed) outcome that they will be found
to be inequitable. Even assuming (and it is a big assumption) that this method
will work, what is supposed to happen to the young women in the class
while their male colleagues articulate their sexism in order to interrogate it?
'Allowing' some students to 'tell their own stories' in public, if those stories
are themselves oppressive, automatically silences others. In his example,
Giroux seems to be privileging a particular (male) voice over those of the
other groups in the classroom; this is precisely what he claims to be fighting
against.

Furthermore, in this situation, 'hierarchies of oppression' can arise (Luke,
1994). Ellsworth (1989), who attempted to put into practice the methods of
critical pedagogy while developing an anti-racist discourse with university
students, found that the presence of one group of students talking of their
oppression could of itself constrain other, differently oppressed groups, to
silence.

> Participants expressed much pain, confusion, and difficulty in speaking,
> because of the ways in which discussions called up their multiple and
> contradictory social positionings. Women found it difficult to prioritize
> expressions of racial privilege and oppression when such prioritizing
> threatened to perpetuate their gender oppression. Among international
> students, both those who were of color and those who were White found
> it difficult to join their voices with those of U.S. students of color when
> it meant a subordination of their oppressions as people living under U.S.
> imperialist policies and as students for whom English was a second
> language. Asian American women found it difficult to join their voices
> with other students of color when it meant subordinating their specific
> oppressions as Asian Americans. I found it difficult to speak as a White
> woman about gender oppression when I occupied positions of institutional
> power relative to all students in the class, men and women, but positions
> of gender oppression relative to students who were White men, and in
> different terms, relative to students who were men of color. (p. 312)

Brown and Gilligan (1993) argue that females are particularly likely to
feel the need to silence their own voices in order to preserve relationship
with others, and that this is especially the case in adolescence. They describe

teenage girls as feeling that they have to 'give up relationship for the sake of "Relationships"' (p. 14). This suggests that girls would be unlikely to risk the good relations of the classroom in order to articulate feelings of oppression by groups represented in the class.

Within oppressed groups, individuals can share some voices while having others in mutual antagonism. Kitzinger (1987), for example, describes the anger expressed by lesbians who had come to such an orientation through feminist separatism and who then found themselves expected to identify with gay men in a mutually-embracing gay consciousness and struggle. The discourse of student voice assumes unproblematically that such complications and contradictions can be avoided by the pedagogue's skilful drawing out of individual consciousnesses. It ignores the way that many oppressed groups are themselves oppressors in other arenas; the sexism of many young working-class men being just one example (McRobbie, 1991; Willis, 1977).

Furthermore, the articulation of oppression in one arena may cut across and cause problems for larger issues of personal and group identity which may be very important to a person's ability to resist other oppressive practices. Fordham (1996), for example, notes the importance to the black students in her study of what she describes as 'fictive kinship', a term used by anthropologists

> to refer to people within a given society to whom one is not related by birth but with whom one shares essential reciprocal social and economic relationships . . . Among Americans of African descent, this connection extends beyond the social and economic to include a political and prestige function as well. (p. 71)

Fordham argues that a key feature of this fictive kinship system has been solidarity within the African-American community, such that 'my brother is my brother regardless of what he does or has done' (p. 98). This group solidarity has been a very important factor in the ability of the African-American community as a whole to maintain a positive identity under oppression, but it has its costs. Fordham argues that it is one reason why many of the students in her study resisted competitive success in school; the fictive kinship system stresses cooperation and group membership over the individualistic competition expected by the school. I would further argue that the group solidarity stressed by such a system would make it difficult, for example, for young black women to articulate feelings about gender oppression by black men. Privileging gender over race in this way would undercut the primary connection to African-American group society, a connection that may well be perceived as essential in order to resist the additional oppression of racism (hooks, 1982). Solidarity within an oppressed group may make it impossible dispassionately to discuss intra-group oppressions. The privileging of reason in the examination of experience fails to take into account the fact that it is only the powerful who are able to suspend the particularities of their experience. Those in the position of Other need to retain a sense of their oppression in order to provide mutual support in the face of this positioning. Because the abstract Subject is a particular version of white, able-bodied masculinity, those who do not have these attributes may find that taking on this Subject position requires too high a price.

Challenging Reason: Gender and Moral Development

I now want to look at a specific challenge to the dominance of reason in Western thought: Gilligan's work on alternative moral voices. Originating in developmental psychology, the earlier studies have been criticized for focusing on too narrow a group of white middle-class girls and women. Arguably, this has positioned them as Subject with relation to a multiplicity of differently raced, classed and abled Others (Greeno and Maccoby, 1986; McNay, 1992; Stack, 1986), although this deficiency has at least been partially addressed in the later research. However, the ideas arising from this body of work have implications both for moral philosophy and for areas of education seemingly far removed from ethical questions.

As I outlined in Chapter 2, Gilligan's study is a critique of the influential developmental stage sequence for moral understanding outlined by Kohlberg. Kohlberg starts from the position that the highest stage in philosophical thought is one in which decisions are governed by universal principles of justice. This position reflects the Kantian tradition in Western moral philosophy, in which it is argued that moral judgments apply disinterestedly between persons and are arrived at by reason applied to non-contextualized cases. Rawls (1972), for example, to whose work Kohlberg's sequence is closely related (Hekman, 1995), outlines a theory of justice in which moral principles are arrived at by hypothetical disembodied subjects; it is assumed that the clearest way to arrive at such principles is to debate them behind a 'veil of ignorance' about the particularities of one's actual life. Given this philosophical starting point, it is not surprising that Kohlberg's developmental sequence follows the line it does. Piaget points out that, rather than being built up from its base in infancy, 'a conception of development instead hangs from its vertex of maturity, the point toward which progress is traced' (Gilligan, 1982, p. 18). So from within a context in which rational, detached judgment is seen as the pinnacle of moral thought, Kohlberg, by tracing the moral development of eighty-four boys over a period of twenty years, developed a stage-based model of how (if at all) they reached this position. The model has six levels, but it has since been suggested that the last two apply only to a very small proportion of even the American male population with whom it was developed (Greeno and Maccoby, 1986).

Kohlberg found, however, that female subjects tended to reach only level 3, in which reasoning

involves a concern with maintaining bonds of trust with others . . . The 'good'
or 'right' action is that which will not hurt those with whom one has valued
relationships. Shared feelings and agreements take priority over individual
interests. (Greeno and Maccoby, 1986, p. 311)

Level 4, to which more males are seen to mature, is concerned with

what might be called . . . a societal level of thought, where moral issues are
considered in terms of a system of law or justice that must be maintained
for the good of society. (Greeno and Maccoby, 1986, p. 311)

Kohlberg argued that the reason why women did not attain the higher
stages of his developmental sequence was that they did not have the experience of civil society necessary to attain this level of moral thought; if they
were encouraged to operate more in the public sphere they would move to
be equal to males (Hekman, 1995). Gilligan, by contrast, argues that it is
inappropriate to treat Kohlberg's sequence as *the* developmental sequence
when it fails to take female experience into account. In attempting to fill the
gap left by Kohlberg's gendered research, she found that the women and
girls she studied articulated a very different way of thinking about moral
questions.

In his research, Kohlberg presented people with moral dilemmas and
considered how they approached their resolution. One of these, discussed
by Gilligan (1982), concerns Heinz, whose wife has a terminal illness. A drug
is available which might cure her, but it is expensive, Heinz cannot afford
it, and the druggist will not take a lower price. The dilemma presented is
whether Heinz should steal the drug in order to save his wife. Gilligan contrasts the responses of two 11-year-old children, Jake and Amy, which she
suggests are typically gendered. Jake accepts the dilemma in Kohlberg's
terms as a question of the competing values of property rights and the right
to life, and is clear that Heinz should steal the drug:

For one thing, a human life is worth more than money, and if the druggist
only makes $1,000, he is still going to live, but if Heinz doesn't steal the
drug, his wife is going to die. (p. 26)

Jake considers the moral dilemma to be 'sort of like a math problem
with humans' (p. 26), and assumes that anyone following his reasoning
would come to the same conclusion. Amy, on the other hand, has a completely
different approach. She is unable to see the Heinz dilemma as a self-contained
problem with only one possible choice of solutions, to steal or not to steal
the drug. But instead treats it as situated within real human relationships.

If he stole the drug, he might save his wife then, but if he did, he might
have to go to jail, and then his wife might get sicker again, and he couldn't

get more of the drug, and it might not be good. So, they should really just talk it out and find some other way to make the money. (p. 28)

Focusing on the context presented and imagining how events might play out within that context, Amy looks for alternative solutions.

She considers the solution to the dilemma to lie in making the wife's condition more salient to the druggist or, that failing, in appealing to others who are in a position to help. (p. 29)

Gilligan sets the response of Amy and others like her alongside her findings from a study of women making decisions about abortion, to suggest that the 'justice voice' of moral theory and male-based moral development is not the only way in which people conceptualize moral problems. She argues that there is a 'different voice' of caring and human connectedness articulated predominantly by girls and women, in which moral dilemmas are characterized not by competing rights but by competing responsibilities within a context of interpersonal care and continuing relationship. The women in her abortion study, for example, frame their dilemmas not in terms of the competing rights of mother and unborn child (as is typical of such debates within traditional moral philosophy) but in terms of the responsibility to self and others with whom one has ongoing relationships.

Gilligan suggests that there are developmental reasons for the two different moral orientations, and that this has again been overlooked by the tendency for those studying child development to use male-only samples or to exclude findings from female subjects when reporting (Kitzinger, 1994b). She argues that separation from the mother is crucial to the formation of masculine gender identity, and is therefore stressed in theoretical work derived from male samples. Following Chodorow (1978) she suggests that girls, on the other hand, experience themselves as like their mothers, and thus have a basis for empathy built into their primary definition of self. In this scheme, masculinity is defined by separation, femininity throught attachment, so it is not surprising that gendered moral orientations reflect these different perspectives on the self (Gilligan, 1982).

Despite these developmental differences, Gilligan is not suggesting that males and females always approach moral dilemmas in different ways, or that such approaches are essential features of women and men. Indeed, subsequent work (Gilligan and Attanucci, 1988) suggests that both sexes are able to use and articulate both moral voices and that, to some extent, the voice articulated by a respondent can be 'cued' by the way a question is presented. The findings of these studies, however, confirm that females are more likely to use the care orientation as their primary way of focusing on moral problems, while males are more likely to take the justice perspective as their starting point. Gilligan and Attanucci (1988) see the two voices as acting in counterpoint, and note that the tension between these perspectives is suggested by the fact that detachment, which is the mark of mature moral judgement in the justice perspective, becomes the moral problem in the care perspective, that is, the failure to attend to need. Conversely, attention to the particular needs and circumstances of individuals, the mark of mature moral judgement in the care perspective, becomes the moral problem in the justice perspective, that is, failure to treat others fairly, as equals. (p. 233)

Gilligan and Attanucci suggest that the tendency of each gender to lose sight of the perspective typified by the other explains the justice focus of studies of moral development. In samples consisting only of males, the caring voice will simply not be heard. While agreeing that this is another instance of the placing of females as Other in developmental psychology, I would also argue that the rationalist bias of Western ethical thought would have made it difficult for anyone starting from Kohlberg's philosophical position to construct a different developmental schema. Indeed, Heckman (1995) notes that many of the women and girls studied by Gilligan were reluctant to label their moral voices as 'moral' at all. It is only when faced by the overwhelming counter-evidence from female-only studies that the degree to which women have been positioned as Other in both the philosophical and psychological traditions becomes clear. It is also increasingly becoming apparent that females are not the only Others in this context; subsequent studies have suggested the possibility of a multiplicity of moral voices, arising from different racial and cultural contexts (Stack, 1986; Hekman, 1990).

Gilligan's work also reflects and complements other studies of gender difference, for example from sociolinguistics (Coates, 1994; Fisher, 1994; Swann, 1992a and b; 1994; Swann and Graddol, 1994). One example of this is Tannen's work on male and female conversational styles. Tannen's writing, particularly in its popular, 'self-help' form, has been criticized by feminist sociolinguists for ignoring power relations, treating gender differences as given rather than the product of social relations, disregarding other factors such as race and social class and locating the potential for change in individuals (in particular, women accommodating the conversational preferences of men) (Cameron, 1995; DeFrancisco, 1992; Kramarae, 1992). Cameron (1995), for example, argues that language styles are themselves produced as masculine and feminine and that individuals make varying accommodations to this in the process of constructing themselves as gendered subjects; talking like a woman is one way of enacting my gender. In doing this I enact and reflect a power relation in which women's voices are produced as less important than men's. While I agree with this critique, and would wish to locate the differences that Tannen (1991) describes in a network of power relations which may well constrain women to develop particular sorts of conversational style, her empirical work supports and expands the arguments put forward in this chapter.

Tannen (1991) suggests that there are significant differences between the way men and women talk. She distinguishes between *rapport-talk*, which is characteristic of women, and *report-talk*, which is mainly used by men. These differences, she argues, reflect fundamentally different approaches to conversation, approaches which closely reflect Gilligan's different moral voices:

> For most women, the language of conversation is primarily a language of rapport: a way of establishing connections and negotiating relationships. Emphasis is placed on displaying similarities and matching experiences . . . For most men, talk is primarily a means to preserve independence and negotiate and maintain status in a hierarchical social order. This is done by exhibiting knowledge and skill, and by holding centre stage through verbal performance such as story-telling, joking, or imparting information. (p. 77)

Tannen's work suggests that the 'different voice' found in females is not confined to moral thinking, but is part of everyday conversational style. Furthermore, she associates rapport-talk with prioritizing connected-ness and report-talk with preserving independence; this reflects Gilligan and Chodorow's hypotheses about differential male and female concepts of the self.

The Implications of Gilligan's Work for Education

A number of implications for education arise out of Gilligan's work. Probably the most important concerns her evidence about the different ways in which males and females respond to problems. Although her ideas have been developed mainly in the contexts of moral choice and personal identity, there are resonances with studies of problem solving in other domains, some of which have been followed up by specialists in these fields.

Tannen (1991), for example, argues that males and females approach talking about personal problems in radically different ways. She suggests that women and girls use 'troubles talk', in which problems are shared and discussed, often at length, as a way of reinforcing interpersonal connection; the conversation, as an expression of solidarity in adversity, is more important than solving the problem. Boys and men, on the other hand, prioritize coming to a solution, and find it puzzling that when a woman says she is troubled by something she does not necessarily want to be told what to do about it. Although this tendency to try and solve problems for women is likely to reflect men's greater access to the wherewithal to enact such solutions, this may also be one reason why, after the age of 16, males predominate in solution-focused mathematics and science subjects and females in the more discursive humanities. It may of course also be a factor in the higher value given, in Western society, to the former areas of study. However, even within

mathematics, differences have been established between the learning preferences of males and females. Boaler (1997) found that, in the schools she
studied, teenage boys were more interested in completing mathematics
exercises than in understanding the techniques being practised. Girls, on the
other hand, were more concerned with understanding than with rapid
completion of the work. Such differences in style are also reflected in the
quotes from Jake and Amy above. Jake is keen to come to a clear-cut answer to
the Heinz dilemma, while Amy talks around the problem, sure that a solution
can be found, but not focusing on finding a definitively 'correct' outcome.
Such early closure on 'the answer' to a problem may be one reason why
adolescent boys often foreclose on stereotypically masculine identities; they
are driven to a 'solution' of the identity crisis of adolescence (see Chapter 8).
It may also have a further connection with the male preference for seeing
moral dilemmas in terms of justice and rights; if you have a rule that you
can always follow, it will mean that it is quicker and easier to resolve ethical
questions in the future.

Gilligan's finding that girls take more account of context when considering moral dilemmas is related to this, and also to gender differences
noted by researchers in science education. Murphy (1990) found that, when
presented with contextualized science problems, girls were more likely than
boys to take seriously the contexts in which they were couched. This is not
surprising in the light of Tannen's work. Taking into account a real human
context makes it harder to come to a clear solution; decontextualizing scientific
and mathematical problems makes unambiguous solutions more attainable.
Unfortunately, because decontextualized reason is seen as a mark of good
scientific understanding, the girls in Murphy's study were regarded by the
assessor as performing less well than the boys, who simply ignored the
context and got on with an abstracted science investigation (Gipps and
Murphy, 1994). In one example,

> students were investigating the load that a model boat would support but
> in the context of a supposed trip round the world. More girls than boys
> decided to investigate the stability of the boat in different conditions i.e.
> monsoons, whirlpools and gales. The girls' actions involving watering cans,
> spoons and hair dryers were interpreted as of a lack of understanding of the
> task rather than of evidence of an alternative task. (Murphy, 1990, p. 6)

Similarly, Amy refuses to address Heinz's dilemma out of its context,
and, on Kohlberg's scale, is considered to be less fully developed morally
as a result. Gilligan (1982) notes that she, too, is addressing an alternative
question:

> Amy's response stems from the fact that Amy is answering a different
> question from the one the interviewer thought had been posed. Amy is
> considering not *whether* Heinz should act in this situation ('*should* Heinz

steal the drug') but rather *how* Heinz should act in response to his awareness
of his wife's need ('Should Heinz *steal* the drug?'). The interviewer takes the
mode of action for granted, presuming it to be a matter of fact; Amy assumes
the necessity for action and considers what form it should take. (p. 31)

Work in mathematics education carried out by Brown and Walter (Brown
and Walter, 1983; Brown, 1986; Walter and Brown, 1977; Walter, 1987a,b)
focuses on this redefinition of problem situations. They argue that Amy is
first 'de-posing' and then 're-posing' the dilemma, and that a similar approach
would be a productive way forward for mathematics teaching. Problem
posing, they suggest, is a crucial adjunct and precursor to problem solving;
the number and kinds of solutions that can be found to a problem depend
at least in part on the way it is posed; this reflects the later work of Gilligan
and her collaborators (Gilligan and Attanucci, 1988; Kitzinger, 1994a). Because
Jake accepts and works within the decontextualized expectations of the
interviewer, he is able to treat Heinz's dilemma as a 'math problem with
humans' (Gilligan, 1982, p. 26) and come fairly rapidly to a single solution.
Brown and Walter argue that approaching even mathematical problems this
way is also unnecessarily limiting. They suggest that mathematical questions
should be 'de-posed', by moving from the question to the situation that
prompted it, in a way analogous to Amy's de-posing of Kohlberg's dilemma.
A fertile approach to solving a problem, they argue, is to look at the
assumptions behind its formulation and then to consider what would be the
consequences if these assumptions turned out to be false. Brown and Walter
(1983) suggest that it is these assumptions which often prevent creative
thinking and successful solutions of longstanding problems in mathematics:

> For a very long time, people tried to *prove* Euclid's fifth postulate [the
> parallel postulate]:
>
>> Through a given external point, there is exactly one line parallel to
>> a given line.
>
> It was only during the past century that we began to realize that the diffi-
> culty in answering the question lay in the assumptions behind the question
> itself. The implicit question was:
>
>> How can you prove the parallel postulate from the other postulates
>> or axioms?
>
> It took hundreds of years to appreciate that the 'how' was an unrecognized
> monster. If you delete the 'how', the question is answerable (in the negative
> it turns out); if you do not do so, the question destroys itself by its excess
> baggage. (pp. 3–4)

In mathematical contexts, de-posing problems is analogous to challenging
the predominance of reason. It undermines deeply held assumptions and
allows other possibilities, other voices to come into the frame.

77

Gilligan's challenge to the dominance of reason in models of moral development is thus shown to be important even for the paradigmatic case of the mastery of reason: the procedures of pure mathematics. It suggests that by hearing only the dominant male voice Western thought has closed off potentially fertile avenues of investigation. Even when we focus on decontextualized reason, we need to be aware of contrapuntal voices of context and connectedness. In doing this we make possible not only the development and valuing of alternative traditions, but also make it clear to ourselves and our students that there are many voices, and that more than one may be 'right'. Taking care to listen to and take into account this multiplicity of voices makes it less likely that we will perpetuate a model in which some groups are perceived as deficient because they have been positioned as Other to a hegemonic male norm. We will also be more likely to be able to develop and recognize the potential and achievement of all our students.

Summary

This chapter has outlined the dominance of reason in Western thought and considered the ways in which this obscures alternative voices. I have shown how the use of reason as the basis for empowerment discourses can of itself be disempowering. I then went on to consider the ways in which a hegemonic rationality has positioned women and other subordinate groups as Other in relation to norms of moral development and looked at an alternative framework suggested by the work of Carol Gilligan. Finally, I considered the implications of this and related studies for educational theory and practice.

Key Points

- Reason is hegemonic in Western thought, with decontextualized knowledge seen as particularly powerful.
- The dominance of reason in discourses of empowerment has in practice been disempowering for particular groups whom it positions as Other.
- Because there are multiple voices, multiple Others, the articulation of one oppression can silence the voices of those oppressed in different ways.
- Gilligan and her collaborators, in looking at how females have been rendered Other by theories of moral development, have found alternative moral voices to those of the dominant rationalist tradition. They suggest that there are multiple moral voices, of which they identify two: that of justice and that of caring and connectedness. This work has been supported by studies in sociolinguistics.
- The work of Gilligan and her colleagues has implications for a number of educational issues outside of moral development, for example,

assessment in science education and issues of problem posing in mathematics classrooms.

Question

In this chapter I have looked specifically at challenges to the dominance of reason in mathematics, science and moral thought. In what other areas does reason hold sway, and how may this be challenged?

Further Reading

GILLIGAN, C. (1982) *In a Different Voice: Psychological Theory and Women's Development*, Cambridge, Massachusetts: Harvard University Press. In this book Gilligan sets out her theory that there is an alternative moral voice. It is very readable, and now considered to be a classic text.

HEKMAN, S.J. (1995) *Moral Voices, Moral Selves: Carol Gilligan and Feminist Moral Theory*, Cambridge: Polity Press, takes the psychological work of Gilligan and her collaborators and applies it to moral philosophy. In doing so she provides a deconstructive critique of the Western moral tradition. Given the complexity of its subject matter, this book is very readable.

✳ WALKERDINE, V. (1988) *The Mastery of Reason: Cognitive Development and the Production of Rationality*, London: Routledge, examines the relationship between power, gender and rationality, with particular reference to discourses of child development. It is closely argued and quite difficult, but worth the effort.

Chapter 7

Some Voices Are More Equal than Others: Subject and Other in the School Curriculum

> If knowledge is power, then some forms of knowledge are more powerful than others. It is no accident that the least powerful forms of knowledge are those taught to the least valued groups of pupils. (Attar, 1990, p. 22)

In schools there is a wide range of voices, reflecting differences not just of gender but of 'race', social class and 'ability'. Some are powerful and more easily heard, some are positioned as Other and, again, this is due to more than just gender. Gender is, however, an important structuring factor in the way schools operate and, in particular, in determining who has power, and for whom the official curriculum is intended. In this chapter I am going to consider how gender roles and gendered subject forms are used to position some subjects, teachers and students as Others within the education system.

One way we can examine the complex nature and interplay of inequalities within schools is to look in detail at who are the Others in this setting, and how their Othering comes about. We considered the female Other in Chapters 2 and 3, and in Chapter 8 we will extend the Othered groups under consideration by looking at some subordinated gender roles and identities. First, however, I want to consider the Others of the curriculum: those subjects and students seen as 'exceptions' when the purposes and content of education are discussed. By exploring which subjects are Other to the dominant school curriculum, and by looking at who studies them, we can see how academic Otherness is constructed within schools, which teachers and which students are in powerful positions in this arena, and how this affects schooling as a whole.

In this chapter I shall mainly focus on secondary education, though I will refer to other sectors from time to time. Although in recent years the UK has seen increasing subject specialism in the primary phase, the issue of differential subject status remains most clearly exemplified at secondary level. As curriculum specialization increases as students get older, it is comparatively easy to see which areas are intended for which groups of students. Tertiary education is only intended for an elite group, so at this stage the differences between curriculum areas are exemplified mainly through what is included and what is excluded. At the same time, it should be noted that there is also a hierarchy of sectors in the education system as a whole, in which primary education is itself positioned as Other in several ways. In England and Wales, for example, less state funding is provided for the education of younger children, and the English and Welsh National Curriculum is structured around the discrete subject areas found in secondary schools, rather than around the integrated approach still favoured by many primary school teachers.

A useful way of approaching an examination of the dominant is to focus on that which is subordinate. By looking at what is common to people and systems positioned as Other we are able to bring to light what is usually taken for granted as normal. That is not to say that we should not put the 'normal' explicitly under examination, and in some contexts (for example, in the area of sexuality and sexual orientation (Richardson, 1996; Wilkinson and Kitzinger, 1993)) this has become an important tool in redressing the balance between Subject and Other. In the school context, however, there has been a longstanding tendency for researchers to focus on high status curriculum areas, ignoring those associated with less powerful forms of knowledge. It is, therefore, illuminating to look instead at what it means for a school subject, and those who study it, to be marginal within the curriculum.

Design and Technology and Physical Education: Life in a Marginal Subject

> I expect that the status that [D&T] holds in other teachers' opinions is quite the same as it was twenty years ago . . . I still feel that people probably feel the same way towards us as they do towards, say, PE. I never minded that, it was never a problem for me. I actually think that technology is of a lower academic status anyway . . . As far as academic status is concerned, I rate it low compared with more important things like English, maths and science.
> (Ravi Korde, CDT teacher, Bursley School, 21 February 1994)

Design and technology (D&T) and physical education (PE) are almost paradigmatic in their positioning as marginal subjects, and both have deeply gendered histories whose legacies remain today. PE is unusual for a low status curriculum area in that it has been the focus of a number of studies on which I draw for my discussion in this chapter. In examining D&T I shall be citing evidence from my own research[1], coupled with a number of studies of its contributor/predecessor subjects: craft, design and technology (CDT) and home economics (HE). These studies suggest that the condition of subject marginality is bound up not only with issues of the comparative status of different kinds of knowledge, but also with images of masculinity and femininity that involve ideas about the body, about social class and about the relationship between power, knowledge and the self.

Both D&T and PE are comparatively recent combinations of what were, explicitly or by default, separate subjects for girls and boys. In the case of D&T, the introduction of the National Curriculum in England and Wales included an attempt to replace CDT, HE and business studies (BS), all of which, while officially open to students of both genders, contained heavy gender imbalances, with a gender-neutral subject originally focused around the design process. PE has, until recently, had separate male and female forms, which emphasized different skills and qualities and required different sorts of training for the teachers involved (Fletcher, 1984; Flintoff, 1993). Of course, sport, especially for boys, has always been important to the ethos of fee-paying and other elite schools. In the state sector, however, where both D&T and PE have been taught for more than 100 years, working class students have been seen as an important client group; in the case of HE and PE the subjects were made compulsory with the intention of improving the health of the poor (Fletcher, 1984; Hunt, 1987; Manthorpe, 1986). It is notable, in this context, that the aim for boys was the improvement of their own health, while that for girls was that they should be better wives and mothers, presumably in order that they might improve the fitness (for military service, among other things) of their husbands and sons (Dyhouse, 1976, 1977).

Gendered Subject Ideologies and the Social Control of the Working Classes

Both CDT[2] and its predecessors, the manual crafts (mainly woodwork and metalwork), and the various forms of HE[3] were explicitly used, throughout this century, as agents of social control. In the mid-nineteenth century a concern for the morals and health of the poor, particularly in the cities (Hunt, 1987; Manthorpe, 1986) led to the introduction of domestic subjects, for girls only, into the elementary schools. The finding that in Manchester 800 out of 11 000 volunteers for the Boer War were unfit for active service raised fears about 'national degeneracy', and the high infant mortality rate was blamed on the ignorance and carelessness of mothers, particularly those working outside the home (a belief that was not borne out by the official figures) (Dyhouse, 1977). A general fear of the potential of the working classes to spread both disease and dissent was combined with the belief that the family would act as a stabilizing force, centred around women as homemakers; the domestic training of young girls was designed to counteract what was seen as a worrying trend in the industrial centres (Dyhouse, 1976). Poverty and malnutrition were attributed to a lack of domestic management skills on the part of working-class women; it was believed that this might be remedied by the introduction of classes in cookery, needlework, cleaning and laundrywork (Porter, 1991; Purvis, 1985), even though the schemes of work employed often had little relevance to the actual living conditions of working-class families (Attar, 1990; Turnbull, 1987). The teaching of domestic tasks in ways that failed to take account of the realities of students' lives not only positioned them as Other with respect to presumed social norms, but was combined with an image of family life to which they were expected to aspire. This regarded poverty as an individual issue, amenable to individual thrift, and the maintenance of a 'respectable' home as an entirely female responsibility.

> The development in schools of what in 1910 one educationalist called 'the domestic arts — *cooking, cleaning* and *clothing*' reveals how persuasive and persistent an ideology of domesticity was in influencing girls' schooling. This ideology suggested that domestic work and love of the home should be the focus of women's lives . . . the progress of domestic subjects shows how the curriculum was moulded to encourage working-class girls to see their primary role as members of society to lie in serving others by sewing, cooking and cleaning, both in their own households, and, as a result of society's 'servant problem', in the homes of others. (Turnbull, 1987, p. 87; emphasis in original)

For working-class males, a parallel ideology underlay the introduction of craft subjects into boys' state education. Although there was a belief that crafts were an essential part of a liberal education (Penfold, 1988), CDT and its predecessors were also associated with the inculcation of moral training and industrious habits. Part of the attempt to control the poor through the hegemony of bourgeois family values was a stress on the importance of regular labour to a respectable life; while the dependent wife remained at home, the husband was expected to labour cheerfully at the tasks that were his lot. Manual training was intended to promote this.

> Manual labour and moral training give an impulse to industrious habits which is not given without them. I have carefully watched the influence such training has on some of the most degraded of society . . . Therefore, I conclude that any system of education unconnected with the manual labour is yet imperfect, and I believe this to be the opinion of most experienced people. (Forss, C. (1835) *Practical remarks upon the education of the working classes*, quoted in Penfold (1988) p. 3)

Along with the introduction of universal elementary schooling came a concern that educating working-class children might cause some to aspire beyond their station. Both manual crafts and the HE subjects had a part to play in counteracting this by encouraging young people to be satisfied with their lot:

> . . . the great thing is to show to the working class the real dignity of labour . . . and to let them feel that it is a far nobler thing to be the head of an engineers shop, or to be a first-rate joiner, or a good mason, than it is to be a poor clerk who has to contend against the frightful competition which exists in that class, and who must appear respectable on the narrowest possible means. ('Technical teaching'. *The Health Education Literature*, **14** (1884), quoted in Penfold (1988) p. 6)

Amongst girls . . . great mistakes are made by their longing to 'better themselves' as they say. And, in one sense, it is quite right that they should have such a wish. But first let them be sure that it is bettering themselves to change merely for higher wages, or to get into a higher family. When the girl who is only fitted for housework thinks that because she has been well educated at school, she ought to be a lady's maid, when the lady's maids wish to be governesses, depend upon it they are not getting on in life. (GRANT, A.R. (1871) *School Managers' Series of Reading Books, V,* London: Weale, quoted in Davin, (1987) p. 147)

The use of HE and CDT subjects as instruments of social reform and control, through the direction of different messages towards male and female working-class students, reinforced the ideology of separate spheres for men and women throughout life. Similar ideologies and effects are inherent in the separate forms of boys' and girls' PE. Male and female forms of PE have continued until very recently, and there remains an ideological split between those (mainly male) teachers who see as their main purpose the fostering of the sporting success of the elite, and those (mainly female) interested in promoting the personal and social development of all students through self-paced individual activities (Sparkes, 1991b). The justification for the introduction of PE into elementary schools in the nineteenth century was, again, a perceived need to improve the health both of military recruits and of future mothers (Fletcher, 1984). Sparkes (1991a) argues that this traditional focus on persuading the individual to adopt a particular lifestyle, with the aim of reducing mortality and morbidity in the population as a whole, remains a major impetus behind health-related fitness programmes. This, he suggests, ignores social structural issues in the health of different social groups, and equates concepts of morality with questions of lifestyle. In a way that parallels nineteenth-century ruling-class perceptions of the causes of poverty, those who lead 'unhealthy lives' are seen as morally lax.

PE and CDT both also have a role in promoting and perpetuating forms of working-class masculinity that are associated with working with and on the body. Although, as I argued in Chapter 4, gender is primarily a social construct, it is attributed on the basis of physical signs and forms. Sherlock (1987) notes that there is social pressure on male PE teachers to demonstrate their masculinity by being big and strong physically, while Sparkes (1991b) points out that the possession of a high level of physical skill is a central aspect of the professional identity of many male PE teachers. Similarly, I found that many male CDT teachers saw excellence at craft skills as fundamental to their identities; this was reflected not only in remarks about their current roles but in reflecting on their schooldays. This teacher, for example, explicitly links his youthful pride in his work to his current curriculum focus:

My mum's house was filled with stuff that I'd made at school. I enjoyed it and it's there forever. That may be just me being very much centred on hand skills. (Ravi Korde, Bursley School, 21 February 1994)

D&T and PE as Low Status Subjects

Of course, the association of both PE and the D&T subjects with the body and manual labour contribute considerably to their low status in the curriculum. Both areas have traditionally been targeted at 'less academic', often working-class and disaffected students, partly because such curriculum divisions keep these groups apart from higher achievers, whose progress might be undermined by the former's distracting presence. In England and Wales, for example, the 1944 Education Act introduced a tripartite system which differentiated between the 'academic' student, who would have a traditional liberal education at a grammar school; those who were considered more suited to the study of science and technology, who would go to technical schools; and the rest, who were considered to be more able to deal with concrete things than with ideas (Thom, 1987) and went to the secondary moderns which were formed (along with primary schools) from the former elementary schools (Penfold, 1988). However, few technical schools were established, leaving most of the secondary-age population, as was in practice the case before the Act, split between the largely middle-class grammar school elite and the largely working-class remainder.

Within this system, the low status of CDT and HE was demonstrated as much by their absence from some parts of the system as by their presence in others. Neither CDT nor HE ever became well established in the universities, despite concerted efforts from practitioners (Attar, 1990; Manthorpe, 1986; Penfold, 1988), and, indeed, teacher education in home economics was generally carried out in separate colleges until the 1970s (Attar, 1990). Before it became a requirement for receiving grants in 1905, the higher status girls' schools in England often did not teach HE at all, their headmistresses arguing that such skills were better learned at home (Dyhouse, 1976). Even when forced to introduce them, these schools often gave domestic subjects low status and inferior facilities, preferring to model their curricula on those of the boys' grammar schools. Only those considered not able enough for more academic studies took practical subjects to examination level. A student at the Park School for Girls in Preston in the 1930s, for example, explained that:

> she 'made bread and marmalade and cakes' for only about twelve months, 'because we were streamed you see, and I wasn't in the cookery stream after the first two years. I went in the Science form, and the Domestic Science was more for the — well when I say lower form, I'm not being derogatory, but some are better with working with their hands and they were streamed accordingly'. (Summerfield, 1987, p. 156)

Meanwhile, housecraft and other domestic subjects were seen as central to the education of girls in secondary moderns (Attar, 1990). A similar differentiation took place regarding boys' craft subjects and, indeed, the boys' grammar schools continued to resist them long after HE had become compulsory for girls.

> Deep seated prejudices against practical work and long memories of the
> pattern and provision for workshop teaching within the old elementary
> school system meant that practical subjects were relegated predominantly
> to the domain of the lowest stratum — the secondary moderns. In Grammar
> schools they were never more than a peripheral activity. (Penfold, 1988,
> p. 112)

With the introduction of comprehensive education, with its ideals of
equal access to all, it might have been expected that there would be an end
to this division between those whose education was academic and whose
was practical. However, what happened in practice was that some students
were encouraged to spend a considerable proportion of their time studying
CDT and HE, while others were not. Riddell (1992), for example, notes that,
even as recently as the 1980s, the high-achieving boys in her study were
channelled out of applied science and technology subjects. Meanwhile, those
considered to be 'less able' have been encouraged, particularly after age 14,
to spend as much time as possible in the CDT and HE areas. One teacher,
for example, explains the reluctance of the former head of her school to
move from CDT and HE to the less practical D&T:

> . . . in this school, that whole area certainly gave him the best results in
> examination level. It also kept him out of an awful lot of trouble because
> a large number of the less able children for example were pushed into that
> area because it was practical. (Sue Pennington, Turnhill Community School,
> 6 January 1993)

In largely working-class schools like Turnhill, such differential curriculum
access did have some advantages for the 'less able' students, some of whom
had their only examination successes in these subjects. There were other
benefits for both schools and staff. Craft subjects continue to make an
important contribution to the public face of many schools, with graphic
design work and completed artefacts being displayed in public areas and at
parents' evenings. The concentration of the 'less able' and disaffected in the
domestic and craft subjects also provided one source of status for the teachers,
who, because of the practical nature of the work, its perceived relevance to
the world outside school, and the less formal relationships possible in a
kitchen or workshop, were often able to succeed with students considered
to be difficult to teach elsewhere in the school. Those students seen as Other
to the dominant model of the academically able, white and often male norm
were successfully contained in subject areas also seen as Other to the
dominant academic curriculum. The move to the less practical D&T, with its
greater design focus and whole-school clientele, while, in theory at least,
raising the status of the contributing subjects, reduced this source of success
and prestige. D&T was intended to be a gender-neutral amalgam of the best
of HE and CDT, with a stronger and more rigorous focus on the design

process to systematize the subject and stretch the more able students. However, not only did the amalgamation between two very gendered subject areas prove difficult in practice, particularly for the staff involved, but the attempt to raise the new subject's status by making it a compulsory 16+ examination subject had a number of unforeseen results. The new subject became increasingly 'masculine' in orientation, in the sense that there was an emphasis on those aspects, originally taught in CDT, that were traditionally associated with males. This was paralleled by increasing male domination of the teaching staff, particularly in terms of promotional opportunities (Paechter, 1993; Paechter and Head, 1996b). At the same time, the increased academic content marginalized the traditional constituency of 'less able' students, who found themselves no better able to cope with this subject than with the rest of the curriculum. The thinking behind the National Curriculum, because it focused on the 'more able' and 'average' students as Subject, failed to deal with the loss, for the less academically successful, of a curriculum area in which they could do reasonably well. As one teacher put it:

> Another subject has been removed from the curriculum that kids look forward to, if they do look forward to it, for enjoyment and pleasure. And now the underachievers in academic subjects underachieve in technology as well . . . And I find that the kids that achieve well in the other subjects achieve well in this one. (Ravi Korde, CDT teacher, Bursley Comprehensive School, 22 April 1993)

With the revisions of the National Curriculum introduced in 1995, D&T, while remaining compulsory, is no longer an examination subject for all. This is likely to mean a move back to a situation similar to that in most schools before the National Curriculum, with 'more able' students being counselled into taking only a 'short course' in the subject after age 14, and the 'less able' being encouraged, once again, to spend more of their time there. This, coupled with the development of associated vocational courses and the flexibility in school timetables to offer subjects such as child development as a GCSE option, is likely to reinstate the position of the D&T subjects as a potential ghetto for working-class and disaffected students. The effect of this is two-edged. While it has some advantages for the students, giving them a space in which they can be successful with teachers who enjoy teaching them, at the same time, it means that they have fewer opportunities to study higher status subjects. It also perpetuates the positioning both of these subjects and of those who teach and learn them as marginal to the dominant purposes of the school.

This differential counselling of the 'more able' out of and the 'less able' and disaffected into lower status subjects also takes place with respect to PE, which, again partly because of its informal nature, can be the only aspect of school that some students enjoy (Templin et al., 1988). It is suggested by some researchers that this is particularly true of young black males. Carrington and Wood (1983), for example, point to the 'colonization' of school sports teams by black students already 'cooled out' of the academic mainstream. They argue that in the school they studied this process was encouraged by teachers, who overlooked poor behaviour from students who were playing in school teams, and was reinforced, through their influence on team membership, by the black students themselves. The importance of PE, and particularly inter-school sporting success, to the school's public image meant that disciplinary concessions were made to keep good athletes committed to playing in school teams. Carrington and Wood (1983) note some of the problems associated with this way of dealing with disaffected students:

> The shortcomings of this coping strategy are self evident: (1) It serves to reinforce both academic failure and unacceptable behaviour. (2) Insofar as the opportunities for success in school sport are restricted, it also denies many non-academic pupils even the consolation of an alternative to academic failure! (3) It can result in an intensification of interracial rivalries and conflict. (p. 38)

This use of PE as a place to keep the disaffected out of trouble has recently become more difficult because of the rise of PE as an examination subject with an academic component. At the same time, the prevalence, among male PE teachers working with such groups, of a perspective on the subject centred around sporting prowess, encourages the development within some schools of a dominant, often partially resistant masculinity which gives status to those individuals with certain bodily forms and behaviours. The hegemony of such masculinities can position as Other boys who do not conform to this image (Parker, 1996b), and keeps girls firmly on the margins of the subject.

Because being able to work successfully with disaffected and 'less able' students has been a source of pride for D&T and PE teachers, there has been a tendency for them to stress the specific importance of their subjects for these groups. This HE teacher, for example, explicitly locates the value of her subject in its ability to develop students' self esteem:

> I think it's a really important subject. I mean, there's a case, one of my pupils last year. A real little scrap in the second year[4] and he came in and made chocolate chip cookies. He went out and his head was five times the size it was when he arrived and he was smiling from ear to ear. His sense of achievement in that lesson was probably the highest sense of achievement he's had all year. And I think that it's a pity that they can't . . . do more of that. You know, just the straightforward cooking, because it does their self respect so much good. (Anita Crawford, Turnhill Community School, 17 September 1993)

While of course it is important for non-academic students to have access to sources of success and self-validation within the school setting, this approach positions the 'less academic' and less interested as Other in terms of curriculum provision; they are the abnormal, for whom the 'normal', academic, diet is considered unsuitable. The emphasis on the particular needs of such groups and the requirement to preserve non-academic options to cater for them consolidates their marginalization while perpetuating the low status of these curriculum areas and ensuring that the 'more able' continue to be counselled out of spending more than the minimum time in them.

Furthermore, the existence in the curriculum of subjects that appeal directly to images of masculinity (Parker, 1996b; Connell, 1987; Willis, 1977) and femininity (McRobbie, 1991) held by working-class teenagers may lead these students to make curriculum choices that not only have conservative social structures as part of their overt and covert content, but also, by taking up their school time, exclude them from pursuing subjects with more value in the academic and employment marketplaces (Riddell, 1992). It also perpetuates a gendered and classed Otherness within the curriculum, as some students are encouraged to take these lower status, gendered subjects, while others are counselled to avoid them.

Students and Subjects as Parallel Others

It seems to me that there is a parallel between the Otherness of marginal subjects in the curriculum, the Otherness of specialists in these subjects and the Otherness of the students that study them. PE is so Other to the dominant academic image of a school subject that it is ignored in otherwise important studies (for example, Riddell, 1992; Arnot et al., 1996). Teachers of D&T and PE, because they are not seen as contributing much to the education of the 'high value', 'more able' students, have relatively weak voices in whole school curriculum negotiation. Sparkes et al. (1990), for example, noted that not only were PE staff regarded by others as having little to contribute to general curriculum debate, but that young PE teachers in particular tended to be unaware of the importance of being able to operate as professionals in the wider school arena. Similarly, many discussions of the school curriculum treat girls, black boys and less able students as Others, outside of the normal scope of the curriculum, and for whom it has to be modified. It is not considered strange that what is supposed to be a curriculum for all is at the same time perceived as being unsuitable for more than half of the students. Where the curriculum is seen to fail certain groups, it is not modified for all students, but just for these special cases.

There is a close relationship between the way that some groups are constructed as Other and attempts to exclude them from particular areas of the curriculum. This can be illustrated by the debates early in the twentieth century about whether domestic science should be promoted as an alternative science curriculum for girls. At this time, the formal and academic nature of school science meant that it was seen as unsuited to the needs of most girls, who were being educated by and large either for household labour or its supervision. Manthorpe (1986) argues that, while some of those proposing an alternative, 'female' science curriculum had the need to reform an over-academic subject as their prime motivation, the move to replace, rather than supplement, science with domestic science was seen by teachers as threatening the newly-won right for girls and young women to study science as equals to men. Although there was a clear need to make school science more relevant to everyday life, to do this for one gender alone clearly placed that gender as an Other for whom the unchanged, high-status male curriculum had to be modified, while at the same time excluding girls from the wider scientific community, as was already happening in the USA (Manthorpe, 1986). This was clearly understood by those working in the middle-class girls' schools, who aspired to provide an education for girls equal, in both intellectual rigour and academic status, to that experienced by their brothers.

> The woman science teachers in the early twentieth century believed, as had their predecessors, that a *different* science education for girls would be regarded as an *inferior* science education. Furthermore, an alternative science for girls based on domestic examples was evidently bound up with particular assumptions about women's place and role in society.... Thus a 'domestic science' could not be accepted by women science teachers or many headmistresses because it intended to create a separate school science for girls. This would have explicit consequences for the future of those girls who intended to go to university.... As in the late nineteenth century the dilemma was between taking the same courses as boys — and thus maintaining the same traditions of science education which had been developed in a male education system — or making science more relevant, which at that time meant linking girls' interests to naturalistic assumptions about their future role. (Manthorpe, 1986, pp. 212–3)

This example brings to the fore an interesting and important aspect of the relationship between gender, status and curriculum subjects. The cases of D&T and PE make it clear that it is quite possible for alternative male and female forms of a subject to develop and flourish more or less independently for decades, even in mixed schools. The subjects where this has happened, however, are those that are themselves Other within the school curriculum; they are of low status, and generally aimed at those, often working-class, students who are seen as 'less able'. Higher status subjects only come in one main form; there are no gendered alternatives. The forms and structures of these subjects, with some modifications, are based on the liberal curriculum originally developed for boys and taken up by the middle-class girls' schools aiming to provide equal access to an academic education. In other words, they are the male conceptions of these disciplines. It is only in subjects that are themselves Other that alternative female forms have been allowed to succeed. Conversely, attempts to establish female forms of higher status subjects, such as the development of domestic science as a genuinely alternative science, were bound to fail. Given the hegemonic nature of the male forms of the academic disciplines, alternative conceptions would not have been given equivalent status with the already established male forms. It has, therefore, not been in the interests of those working with girls, particularly with those of academic aspirations, to mount a challenge to the dominance of particular subject cultures. In the struggle to allow at least some girls to become Subjects rather than Others in the academic world, it has been necessary to maintain a parallel male domination of school knowledge forms.

Summary

This chapter has considered the Othering of particular voices within school, focusing in particular on low status curriculum areas. In it I show how low status subject areas have become ghettos for some groups of students, particularly the 'less able' and the disaffected. I have argued that it is only in low status subjects that gendered forms have been allowed to flourish, with the male forms of high status areas having a hegemony that has so far been impossible to challenge.

Key Points

- In schools there is a wide range of voices, but some are more powerful than others. Gender is often important in determining who has power and for whom the most powerful areas of the curriculum are intended.
- There are important parallels between the Otherness of marginal subjects in the school curriculum, such as D&T and PE, and the Otherness of those students who are encouraged to study them.
- Subject marginality is bound up not only with the comparative status of different kinds of knowledge, but also with images of masculinity and femininity that involve ideas about the body, social class, and the relationship between power, knowledge and the self.
- D&T subjects, and both male and female forms of PE have long histories of being used as agents of social control, especially of the poor. Both areas have tended to reinforce the ideology of separate spheres for men and women.
- These subjects have also traditionally been aimed at 'less academic', often working-class and disaffected students, who are counselled into such areas and out of more academic courses. PE has had a particular role as a 'ghetto' for disaffected black males.
- While giving such students areas of the (otherwise largely academic) curriculum in which they can do well, this positions them as Other to mainstream curriculum provision; emphasizing the need to preserve non-academic options for such students maintains their marginalization.

- It is only in marginal subjects that separate gendered forms have been allowed to flourish. In higher-status academic subjects there is only one dominant form; that deriving from the male liberal curriculum tradition.

Question

What is the status of subjects like music, which are marginalized but comparatively academic? How are they gendered, and who studies them?

Further Reading

ATTAR, D. (1990) *Wasting Girls' Time: The History and Politics of Home Economics*, London: Virago Press, is an empirically-based attack on HE as taught in the late 1980s, which argues that, throughout its history, the teaching of HE to girls has had the effect of excluding them from more powerful areas of the curriculum.

FLETCHER, S. (1984) *Women First*, London: The Althone Press, is an interesting history of girls' PE in the nineteenth and twentieth centuries.

RIDDELL, S.I. (1992) *Gender and the Politics of the Curriculum*, London: Routledge, while ignoring PE, does give an excellent account of the ways in which different students are channelled into and out of different school subjects according to teachers' perceptions of both themselves and the students.

Notes

1   I shall be using evidence from two studies. The first, for my PhD (Paechter, 1993) was carried out during the academic year 1990–91, the first year of the introduction of D&T. The second study took place between 1992 and 1994, and was funded by the Economic and Social Research Council (ESRC number R000233548). It was based at the School of Education, King's College, London, and co-directed by John Head and myself. In both studies, the names of teachers, advisory staff and schools have been replaced by pseudonyms.

2   Although CDT is a relatively recent configuration, I am using it as a convenient shorthand for a variety of 'boys' craft subjects, including its predecessor subjects, woodwork and metalwork.

3   I am using 'HE' here to refer to all the domestic subjects (food, textiles, child development, housecraft, laundrywork, etc.), although they have singly and as a group been referred to by a number of names since the nineteenth century. Throughout this period, though the content has changed from time to time, their association with women's work has not, and the teaching staff remains overwhelmingly female.

4   Year 8, age 12–13 years.

Chapter 8

Subordinated Femininities and Masculinities in Secondary Schools

In the 1972 New Hampshire Presidential primary, Senator Edmund Muskie, then the Democratic front-runner, committed political suicide when he publicly cried during a campaign speech. Muskie had been talking about some harsh press comments directed at his wife when the tears filled his eyes. In retrospect it was a watershed moment: Could a man who became tearful when the going got rough in a political campaign be expected to face the Russians? . . . Media accounts of Muskie's all-too-human tears were merciless. (Brownmiller, 1984, p. 163)

On September 29, 1990, a ten-year-old soccer goalie named Natasha Dennis was asked to pull her pants down. Two fathers of opposing players couldn't believe that a girl could be as good as Natasha. She might be a boy in disguise, they contended. (Burton-Nelson, 1994–5, p. 20)

Introduction

Women and men can inhabit and adopt a variety of femininities and masculinities. Some of these confer prestige and power, others are stigmatized and subordinate. This chapter considers three kinds of subordinated masculinities and femininities. First, I look at what it means to resist being a stereotypically macho male, and consider what is at stake for young men attempting to live outside dominant forms of masculinity. I then go on to discuss a group of girls and young women often regarded as being outside of the feminine: those who excel at physical education and sports. Finally, I consider the situation of lesbian and gay students and teachers. These individuals have to survive in the largely homophobic world of the secondary school, while inhabiting masculinities and femininities that do not conform to compulsory heterosexuality.

Subordinated Masculinities

Masculinity may be thought of as a social construction about what it means to be male in certain times and certain places. Masculinity is constructed by various meaning-making practices or systems of representation in various social settings. Such settings include schools, the family, and other 'intimate' social groupings: the workplace, fields of leisure and pleasure, and more broadly, the state. These settings and their discourses on masculinity offer a range of ways of being male but separately and together privilege some as superior. (Kenway, 1996, p. 449)

Most of this book focuses on the female Other in education. In this section, however, I want to consider briefly how some groups of males are constructed as Other in secondary schools. Such groups inhabit and personify subordinated masculinities, whose marginalization by hegemonic forms of masculinity is related to the Othering of girls and women. Hegemonic masculinity can be described as:

a particular variety of masculinity to which others — among them young and effeminate as well as homosexual men — are subordinated. (Carrigan et al., 1985, p. 587)

This subordination functions in many cases through an association of such relatively powerless masculinities with aspects of the perceived feminine.

Masculinities (and femininities) are multiple and contested. Alternative masculinities are not simply different ways of enacting one's maleness. Because of the unequal power relation between women and men, for the latter the maintenance of hegemonic masculinity becomes very important. Those who can identify themselves and be identified by others as archetypally male will accrue extra power to themselves, power which, because it is inherent in the hegemony of this masculinity, is hidden and therefore comparatively unresisted. Of course, what forms of masculinity are dominant will vary between different cultures and contexts. Hegemonic masculinity is always contested; the hegemonic group has to defend its position against rival contenders. Masculinities are thus defined not just in contraposition to femininities, but also against each other. Those not in the dominant group are, in order to preserve that dominance, defined as Other, as not real men (Buchbinder, 1994).

Both this struggle for dominance and the means by which it is established are important aspects of the construction of masculinities (Connell, 1987). Because the power relation between men and women is naturalized as 'normal', it is often obscured and therefore unchallenged. This makes the use of power much simpler for members of hegemonically masculine groups. Because their power is taken for granted, it does not have to be overtly displayed or established (Pyke, 1996). So hegemonic masculinity can confer not just power but the ability to exercise that power unseen. Furthermore, because the naturalization of hegemonic male power arises from male-female social inequalities, the subordination of alternative forms of masculinity is more easily accomplished by positioning subordinate groups as feminine

Others (Back, 1994). This is a twofold process. By attributing feminine characteristics to already subordinated groups, hegemonic masculinities are able to regard their dominance as being a special case of the power of masculine over feminine. At the same time, by enforcing the subordination of masculinities that exhibit 'feminine' characteristics, such as nurturant behaviour, the distance, and thus the power differential, between masculine and feminine is preserved (Kenway, 1996). The feminine man is subordinated, because if he were not, there would no longer be a naturalized justification for the power of men over women. At the same time, the use of female terms (girlie, sissy, woman) to label subordinate male groups (Salisbury and Jackson, 1996) is itself an indicator of the pervasiveness and persistence of power differentials in gender relations.

In discussing subordinated masculinities it is important to remember that this subordination is mainly established with respect to other masculinities (Connell, 1987; Carrigan et al., 1985). Even subordinated males may still be dominant *vis-à-vis* women, particularly women in the same socially marginalized group (Kenway, 1996; Donaldson, 1993). This means, of course, that women's struggles for equality, especially with men, can themselves be sidelined while men battle with each other for dominance, both of women and of other men. For example, hooks, complains that:

> The labelling of the white male patriarch as 'chauvinist pig' provided a convenient scapegoat for black male sexists. They could join with white and black women to protest against white male oppression and divert attention away from their sexism, their support of patriarchy, and their sexist exploitation of women. Black leaders, male and female, have been unwilling to acknowledge black male sexist oppression of black women because they do not want to acknowledge that racism is not the only oppressive force in our lives. . . . people are absolutely unwilling to admit that the damaging effects of racism on black men neither prevents them from being sexist oppressors nor excuses or justifies their sexist oppression of black women. (hooks, 1982, pp. 87–8)

Furthermore, the subordination of some groups of men can lead directly to overt oppression of women from these same groups. Because of the association of subordinate status with femininity, males from less powerful groups have to establish their masculinity in other ways. Pyke (1996), for example, describes how working-class males may enact a hypermasculinity centred around physical labour, sexual prowess and misogyny in an attempt to reconstruct their position as embodying 'true' masculinity (see also Willis (1977)). She also notes that ruling-class men benefit from this both directly and indirectly. They 'demonstrate' their superiority by overtly distancing themselves from such displays, while at the same time gaining power, by association, from media images of embodied male athleticism. The use of particular embodied styles to assert masculinity in the face of a socially subordinate position is also common among young black men both in the

UK`and the US. Such displays can range from particular kinds of stance and movement to clothing, hairstyle and handshake (Gillborn, 1990; Parker, 1996a). hooks argues that the image of the black American male as 'effete, emasculated, crippled' (hooks, 1982, p. 88) also leads to a desire among young black men to prove their masculinity through violence.

A key mechanism in the Othering of subordinated masculinities is their association with femininity (Back, 1994). As explained above, this is largely to do with patterns of domination and subordination between men and women. However, at adolescence, a time when masculinity is experienced as especially precarious, competition between masculinities is also connected to the need of young men to consolidate their gender and sexual identities. In this context, the definition of male as 'not female' is especially salient. Young men unsure of their masculinity will want to draw a clear boundary between themselves and others they perceive as less masculine. Subordinated groups of males in secondary schools are therefore subjected to strong exclusionary pressures, as particular versions of masculinity compete for dominance.

What forms of masculinity become hegemonic is particular to particular cultures, and schools are no exception to this. The forms of masculinity constructed as dominant in secondary schools are not always those with power in the wider society (Redman, 1997). For example, because adolescent masculinity is so precarious, overt demonstrations of masculinity have more salience here than at other times (Walker, 1988). This means that forms of masculinity centred around physical prowess, which may be enacted directly in the form of violence or the threat of violence, are even more important and pervasive in schools than elsewhere (Connell et al., 1982). Parker (1996b) notes that violence is a critical component in the lives of many adolescent boys, and identifies PE as a key site of its enactment. In the school he studied, violence was taken for granted as an element of PE, with specific groups taking advantage of the space and informality of the subject to use what he terms 'gladiatorial violence' to support their own dominant form of masculinity and marginalize others. Those who lacked sporting prowess were seen as effeminate. In this particular case the dominance of a violent masculinity seems to have been more or less complete. The 'victims', boys who identified with the academic norms of the school, did attempt to construct an alternative masculinity around academic achievement. However, not only was this difficult to achieve owing to the classroom disruption of the 'hard boys', but also their conspicuous hard work drew further attention to the 'victims'' deviance. They were bullied into doing the 'hard boys'' work for them.

Mac an Ghaill (1994b) argues that the official curriculum is central in making available a variety of versions of masculinity for students to inhabit. However, the degree to which this is the case will vary from school to school. While Kessler et al. (1985) suggest that streaming can lead to the development of a top-stream masculinity geared to academic achievement, this will not be a universal occurrence. Walker (1988), for example, describes an Australian urban boys' high school in which a 'footballer culture' was dominant. He argues not only that this culture imposed on other groups its particular definition of what it means to be a man, but also that, despite the presence of a variety of elaborated ethnic cultures, there appeared to be no clearly articulated alternative to the dominant stipulation of acceptable male behaviour.

> Together with the cultures of the Greek group and other 'strong' males, the footballer culture tended to impose on other groups and individuals, with varying degrees of penetration, its definition of what it is to be a man. The material outcome of this is the assertion of a monopoly on achieved manhood, through the claim to exclusive possession of legitimate 'knowledge' of how men act. (p. 5)

What this means is that for groups who cannot or do not want to fit the dominant form of masculinity, life can be very hard (Askew and Ross, 1988). Walker (1988) describes, for example, the struggle of 'three friends' in his research school to resist stigmatization as 'poofs' and to develop and sustain masculinities alternative to the dominant 'footballer' culture. The three eventually established at least some right to be different, partly because they were given some private space by a sympathetic teacher, which somewhat protected them from bullying, and partly because they were able to use their alternative culture, developed outside the school around amateur dramatics, to attract respect through the mounting of a successful theatre performance. Walker (1988) points out, however, that this fortunate outcome was achieved only after a long and difficult struggle, and that such struggles are partly against internalized subordination.

> When you are a member of a group whose major problem at school is to handle being defined as 'poofs', taunted and abused by more powerful groups, you are exercising the options of an oppressed group. The classic, and basic problem of oppressed groups is to eject 'the oppressor within'. . . . to refuse your acceptance, as part of your own identity, of stigmatizing definitions as inferior, deviant, or morally deficient. This is at the core of the struggle for cultural autonomy. . . . The three had a . . . difficult and bitter struggle. The hostility they had to handle came from opponents who were, for the moment at least, much stronger than they. (p. 15)

All of this, of course, has implications for changing dominant masculinities. To a certain extent, the model of hegemonic masculinity acts against the interests of certain groups of men. The focus on manual labour in some working-class hypermasculinities can act directly against the long-term interests of young men for whom this is an important identity; in a world in which 'traditional' male jobs are disappearing and credentials have become increasingly important, glorifying manual work is likely to lead to unemployment, which itself undercuts such masculinities (Willis, 1977; Mac an Ghaill,

1994b; Willott and Griffin, 1996). Similarly, the culture of 'effortless achieve-ment' (Mac an Ghaill, 1994b) among some middle-class male groups may cause problems for them if, for example, entry to higher education becomes more competitive (though, given that this seems to be a mainly ruling-class masculinity, it may be that these young men's otherwise privileged position will protect them from failure in the long term).

On the other hand, there are significant disadvantages for both individuals and groups in adopting alternative masculinities. Hegemonic masculinities consolidate unequal power relations between men and women, by positioning both women and subordinate male groups as a feminine Other. For men to change, to become less violent and more nurturant, for example, is for them to take on 'feminine' characteristics; this will lead to a loss of power with respect both to women and to other men. The humiliation of young men inhabiting non-hegemonic masculinities makes the adoption of such alternatives a singularly unattractive prospect. Teenage boys who do not parade their masculinity, those for example who are non-violent, friendly rather than oppressive to girls, not overtly and publicly heterosexual, or quiet and hard-working, have a rough time at school. Enacting an alternative masculinity can be problematic even for younger children. Thorne (1993) noted that primary-aged boys who played girls' games seriously (rather than disruptively) were stigmatized as 'sissies'. Orbach (1993) describes what happened to her 5-year-old son.

> On first starting school he said, 'Well I'm extremely nervous but I suppose all the other children will be too'. A few days later he reported that they (the boys) might be nervous but they showed it by bashing one another up. The following week he said regretfully to his father, 'I'd like to be a gentle boy Dad, but I just don't think I can manage it'. (pp. 48–9)

For some, an alternative masculinity is still necessary or important, and so persists despite peer pressure (Walker, 1988). But for those who feel that a hegemonic masculine role remains an option, what incentive is there for them to be otherwise (Redman, 1996)?

It may be that, if we want to change the power relation between men and women, dominant and subordinated masculinities, we need to stop focusing on masculinities and look instead at men's practices. Hearn (1996) suggests that the recent upsurge of interest in masculinity has focused attention away from what men actually do; instead of thinking about changing their behaviour, men wrestle with their masculinity. The idea that men's practices are the result or expression of their masculinity suggests that changes in behaviour require deep changes in the psyche; if we believe this we are more likely to hold back our impatience at the slow pace of change, and to give men credit for *trying* to change themselves, even if there is little to show for their efforts. Furthermore, Hearn argues, the emphasis on variety and difference in masculinities obscures the core power relation; just because there are multiple masculinities this does not mean that there has been a diminution of domination and oppression.

Focusing on masculinities diverts attention from women and from gendered power relations, and allows those resistant to feminism to claim themselves to be oppressed (Kenway, 1996). At the same time it suggests that different masculinities are genuinely equal alternatives, when they manifestly are not. It is much more difficult for a young man in school to be gentle, gay, or even to have female friends, than it is to be domineering, violent and misogynist. Boys who behave well to girls (even if they remain to some extent dominant over them) are marginalized. In the interests of the girls, as well as of themselves, such comparatively egalitarian behaviour needs our support.

Sporty Girls

Femininity, as constructed in Western culture, is characterized by passivity. As Other, the female is acted upon by the male subject, the unresisting object of his gaze (Berger, 1972). Girls who do not fit this stereotype, by virtue of their athleticism and sporting prowess, are in an anomalous and partially contradictory situation (Carroll, 1986). Sport as an institution is a powerful contributor to the construction of hegemonic masculinity. The importance of the idea of male physical superiority to the construction of hegemonic masculinity means that strong, fit women represent an explicit threat to male dominance (Johnston, 1996). Hence, women and girls who take sports seriously face considerable exclusionary pressure from the men who dominate sporting bodies and everyday practices (Fasting, 1987). 'Female' sports are taken less seriously than those played by men (even when the game is the same, as in soccer, women's participation is virtually ignored) (Bryson, 1987), and females are explicitly excluded from some sports. At the same time, women and girls who do take part in sporting activities may well find their femininity under challenge (Coles, 1994–5; Lenskyj, 1987). While positioned as female in most social interactions, sporty girls also have some of the bodily features and stances of hegemonic masculinity. This 'double' identity has implications for how they construct their own gender and how the form of femininity they develop impacts on the masculinities and femininities of others (Dewar, 1990).

Although even young girls have been found to be involved in fewer aggressive, physically adventurous and competitive activities than boys (Leaman, 1984), and although even in the primary school boys' games tend to dominate the curriculum playground space and extra-curricular opportunities (Williams, 1993), the real contradiction between sporting prowess and femininity comes with puberty. Adolescence is a particularly important period in the relationship between bodily forms and gendered behaviour. During this time, the physical manifestations of sex and sexuality become increasingly apparent, both to the individual and to the wider social group in which s/he is situated. As they go through adolescence, girls may, as part of the process of taking on an overtly feminine role, redefine their relationship to physical exercise (Inner London Education Authority, 1984). Shilling (1992) notes that, in this context, mixed sex sport has added risks for girls, as competitiveness confirms masculinity, not femininity.

Religious and cultural restrictions on forms of dress and modes of behaviour may also start to come into conflict with the expectations for secondary school teachers, for example, that shorts be worn of physical education (PE) (Scraton, 1993). In schools where such prohibitions are insufficiently allowed for, this may result in young women from particular ethnic or religious groups avoiding PE altogether (Carroll and Hollinshead, 1993; Siraj-Blatchford, 1993). Girls may also assert their mature femininity by requesting excusal from games during menstrual periods, thus 'celebrating' the menarche by a withdrawal from physical activity (Leaman, 1984). In doing so they forgo the opportunity to develop 'physical capital' (health, fitness and physical expertise) (Shilling, 1992), in the interests of a more secure feminine performance. Against this background, adolescent girls and women who are active in PE and sports are seen, in many ways, as being outside, or contradictory to, the feminine (Sherlock, 1987; Bloot and Browne, 1996; Sikes, 1988).

A major factor in the perception of sporty girls as anomalous comes directly from their physical presentation. Physically active young women are strong, fit and muscular, a stereotypically masculine embodiment (Johnston, 1996; Connell, 1995). Berger (1972) points out that:

> A man's presence is dependent on the promise of power which he embodies. If the promise is large and credible, his presence is striking. . . . A man's presence suggests what he is capable of doing to you or for you. (p. 45)

Sporty girls, and the women PE teachers who are often their role models, have a similar presence to that of the power-embodying male; their bodies promise action. They are embodied not as objects of the gaze, but as subjects, equipped for physical activity by the development of their muscles; this undercuts their attempts to present themselves as female (Coles, 1994–5; Dewar, 1990). At the same time, it contrasts with their social positioning as feminine. Their bodies may promise physical power, but they are not accorded the social power and prestige awarded to physically powerful males (Humberstone, 1993).

While physical strength and fitness are sources of pride for sporty girls, the establishment and performance of their femininity remains important both for themselves and for others. These therefore have to occur in other ways than directly through bodily forms. In part, they are supported in this by gendered divisions within school sports, which perpetuate the image of the (comparatively) feminine woman. Many girls' games (netball, for example) are 'feminized', less physically demanding, versions of male sports (Fletcher, 1984; Fasting, 1987; Scraton, 1986). Girls and young women remain excluded from contact sports, with the protection of the reproductive organs (in fact, unlike those of males, safely located in the natural defensive structure of the pelvis) sometimes cited as a reason for this (Flintoff, 1993; Scraton, 1986). The historical development of PE has been almost totally gendered, with different male and female versions emerging out of different approaches and training (Fletcher, 1984; Flintoff, 1993). Even in recent years, women's PE has retained an emphasis on lady-likeness and decorum (Sherlock, 1987; Scraton, 1986), and there remains an alternative, super-feminine role associated with gymnastics and dance (Sikes, 1988; Thomas, 1991). Dance, in particular, is a physical activity in which the male gaze is still able to operate in the traditional manner (Sherlock, 1987).

Sporty girls perform their femininity in a social world. In it, femininity and masculinity are constructed in opposition to each other. Within PE this constructive process supports the development of particular forms of femininity and masculinity. For a sporty young woman to be able to see herself as feminine, she needs to be able to contrast herself with masculine counterparts. Her male peers, althletic young men, exhibit the bodily forms of hegemonic masculinity; these provide at least some contrast against which to define her gender identity and role. Dewar (1990), studying a North American degree programme, found that those female althletes who took no trouble to perform femininity were marginalized as 'butch' or 'lesbian' by other students. Sherlock (1987) notes that the female trainee PE teachers she studied were concerned to assert their femininity, and in order to enhance the contrast between themselves and their male colleagues, put pressure on the latter to be extra-masculine. Such pressure is likely to be reciprocal. In order to preserve their difference from women and therefore their power, male PE students and teachers may well require hyper-masculinity of each other, as well as overt heterosexual femininity of their female counterparts (Dewar, 1990). This may also be a partial explanation of the extreme resistance to dance found by Flintoff (1993) among male PE students; the marking of dance as feminine may be of importance to both genders. Lenskyj (1987), Dewar (1990), Sparkes (1994) and Griffin (1992) have also identified pressure on young sportswomen to demonstrate not just femininity but heterosexuality. Griffin argues that the widespread homophobia in American athletics (for example, some coaches have explicit no-lesbian policies) combined with the transgressive image of the female athlete, has led to a culture in which sportswomen are under considerable pressure to demonstrate an overtly feminine heterosexuality. Lesbian athletes are thus further marginalized. Lenskyj notes that many women's sports and fitness magazines emphasize a glamorous heterosexuality and that even female bodybuilding competitors are judged in part according to their heterosexual attractiveness. Coles (1994–5) and Johnston (1996) report that many top bodybuilders, faced with the loss of breast tissue along with other body fat, feel compelled to have breast implants to preserve their 'feminine' bodily presentation. In this sense, sport has been co-opted into the service not only of hegemonic masculinity but of compulsory heterosexuality.

At the same time, sporty girls are supported in the development of a physically assertive femininity by a community of older women PE teachers and student teachers. There is a long tradition of encouraging athletic girls to develop their activities further, usually, given the few opportunities for women to become sporting professionals, through training to teach PE. Although under pressure and scrutiny owing to homophobic fears of all-female groups (Griffin, 1992), this tradition gives these young women a reference group of people on which they can model their femininity without giving up their love of sport. At the same time, it inducts and channels them into a particular career path, which may not be in the best interests of the individual. One former PE teacher (interviewed as part of the study of D&T reported in Chapter 7) described her experience of this process:

> I think when you're sort of sporty, as a young woman you spend a lot of time with other women. Who've been to college and now . . . they're the ones that look as though they have their independence, they have their own cars or flats or whatever. And you just spend a lot of time, you know . . . you just want to do the same and they want to help you. . . . The seniors coach, and some of them umpire, they take you to your matches, and most of them are teachers at the schools anyway. So when you go and play another match, . . . you come across them, and, I don't know, you just feel like you're in the crowd or something. In with them, and they tell you what their college is like and you go there. (Claudia Nightingale, Longshaw Girls' School, 11 October 1993)

In this case, the support network, paradoxically, both encouraged Claudia and held her back; the process of induction into the profession (referred to by her as 'following on') was limited in its horizons. While allowing her to 'convert' her physical capital to cultural capital (Shilling, 1992), it at the same time inhibited the further development of that cultural capital. From her grammar school, Claudia went to PE college to do a lower-level training, while her less athletic friends went to university:

> I don't think I actually looked at any alternatives. I was sort of virtually adopted by the PE teacher and headteacher and I was going to go to PE college, and that was how it happened and I ended up there . . . I was to follow in [my PE teacher's] footsteps or whatever. Yes, it was just sort of an automatic thing that was going to happen, and it did happen and I came out the other end a PE teacher slightly dazed that I was actually a teacher *and* a PE teacher, having not looked at any alternatives really. But quite happy. I mean, I knew I wanted to work outside, I loved my sport, and so it didn't seem a bad thing . . . So then . . . in my last year at PE college I was advised to, because it was a non-degree course (PE was just a Certificate at

the time), I was advised to go and do the extra year at Cambridge and do the B.Ed honours. But part of the pattern of following through was continuing, and it had always been decided that, if one of the other girls' high schools came up in my particular area, then I would go for that job because it would be part of the following on, and, of course, it did. So I went for the job and got it and didn't go to Cambridge. (Claudia Nightingale, Longshaw Girls' School, 11 October 1993)

Because it supports the development of what, despite its embodied power, is a subordinated and sometimes precarious femininity, the sporting sorority has significant effects on the lives and careers of its members, supporting them while simultaneously channelling their ambitions in particular directions.

Lesbians and Gay Males in School

We live in a homophobic society, and the culture of schools is no exception to this. In schools, however, those with gay and lesbian identities are under extra pressure. Throughout the 1980s and 1990s there have been a series of moral panics about gay and lesbian teachers, it being suggested in particular that the presence of such people working with adolescents in schools will have an effect on the sexualities and sexual orientations of these young people. This has meant, among other things, that lesbian and gay teachers have for the most part been unable to be out at school, rendering them invisible in an institution central to young people's lives. For lesbian and gay teenagers, coming to terms with a sexual orientation which does not fit into the prevailing heterosexual stereotypes for masculine and feminine identities can exacerbate the already difficult period in which a young person has to work out who they are, where they stand and what they believe in (Head, 1997).

Although some lesbian and gay teachers have reported that the students in their schools have been more ready to accept them than have their colleagues (Melia, 1996; Mills, 1996; Rensenbrink, 1996; The Gay Teachers' Group, 1987) secondary school students, especially boys, police each other's gender and sexual identities closely. Fear and prejudice around homosexuality in schools is related, as it is in the wider society, to compulsory heterosexuality as part of normalized forms of gender identity and role. For boys, in particular, homophobia is an important mechanism by which they police the boundaries of masculinity and femininity. This is apparent in the ways that homophobic name-calling is used to restrict the behavioural styles of both male and female students; 'queer', 'gay', 'poof' and 'lezzie' are all used as terms of abuse in the stigmatization of subordinated masculinities and femininities (Parker, 1996b; Lees, 1993; Waldner-Haugrud and Magruder, 1996). That such abuse comes especially from boys is related once again to their need to draw a clear distinction between masculinity and femininity in order to retain and justify male power. The force of compulsory heterosexuality means that gay men have to be seen as feminine, and non-hegemonic masculinity is equated with gayness[1].

> Gayness, in patriarchal ideology, is the repository of whatever is symbolically expelled from hegemonic masculinity, the items ranging from fastidious taste in home decoration to receptive anal pleasure. Hence, from the point of view of hegemonic masculinity, gayness is easily assimilated to femininity. (Connell, 1995, p. 78)

Parker (1996b) notes, for example, that the 13–14-year-old boys in his study used homophobic terms of abuse against those who performed badly in competitive sports, were friendly with girls, or even talked for any length of time with female teachers. He suggests that:

> in the case of the boys at Coleridge, in calling someone a 'poof', pupils were not implying that certain individuals were in fact gay. Rather, this term, and others like it (i.e. 'fag', 'faggot' and 'queer'), were implicitly conceptualised in terms of gender as opposed to sexuality, and therefore constituted some kind of gender-structured generic, meaning 'non-masculine', or 'effeminate'. (p. 149)

It would seem, then, that for boys in their early teens, conformity to masculine stereotypes is more salient than actual sexual orientation. Similarly, 'lezzie' is used, again by boys, as a term of abuse directed at girls, whatever their sexual preference, who do not conform to feminine stereotypes (Lees, 1993). It must be noted, however, that the abusive force of these terms is of course derived from homophobia; the reason that it can be oppressive to be called 'gay' or 'lesbian', whether you are or not, is that lesbians and gay men are, in fact, stigmatized both in and outside school.

This prevailing atmosphere of homophobia, and what Epstein and Johnson (1994) refer to as 'the heterosexual presumption' (p. 198) make it very difficult for young lesbians and gay men in school. They have to find ways of establishing gender and sexual identities outside of the regime of compulsory heterosexuality, and in circumstances where role models are often absent or inaccessible. Although most schools probably have at least one gay or lesbian teacher, in most cases they will not be out, at least to the students (Griffin, 1991; Warren, 1984). Lesbians and gay men are almost totally absent from the curriculum, except as problems; while the rampant heterosexuality of certain historical figures, for example, may be commented on, the homosexuality of others is ignored (Warren, 1984; Trenchard, 1984). In some ways the inclusion of HIV/AIDS education has exacerbated this marginalization; gay men and homosexual behaviour are now present, but in relation to risks of serious infection, and lesbians remain absent.

A particular issue for lesbians and gay men in school, both teachers and students, is the fact that while homophobic attitudes make public acknowledgment of one's sexual orientation a difficult and dangerous option, keeping it secret also has considerable personal cost. Being in the closet means not just silence about one's sexuality, but evasion or denial about large parts of the rest of one's life. For gay and lesbian teachers, for example, it means not being able to take part in staffroom gossip about weekend activities, not being able to bring one's partner to school social functions and, in extreme cases, having to go through relationship breakup or the death of one's partner without any institutional support or bereavement leave (Griffin, 1991; Melia, 1996; Sullivan, 1993). Lesbian and gay students may find it difficult to join in the general talk about sexual conquests or 'who fancies whom', and may have to deal with the ups and downs of adolescent relationships (including unreciprocated love for straight friends) without the support of either their friends or their parents. For both teachers and students, the need to remain closeted in school can also be experienced as a denial of one's 'real' self. Sparkes (1994), for example, in discussing the situation of a lesbian PE teacher whose life history he has studied, writes of:

> Jessica's daily struggle to maintain the integrity of her substantial self, and the ways she is forced to manage her lesbian identity, in situations characterized by varying degrees of homophobia. . . . That Jessica in her present position as a PE teacher . . . has to constantly maintain a split between her personal and professional life for fear of losing her job, highlights the manner in which heterosexism and homophobia operates to oppress her and many other teachers. (pp. 98–9)

The resulting invisibility of lesbian and gay men in most schools is of course part of a vicious circle; it means that there are few role models for young people and little structural support for gay and lesbian teachers, which of course makes it more difficult for either teachers or students to come out at school (Melia, 1996; Warren, 1984; Sanders and Burke, 1994).

Of course, all marginality is relative, and some gay men and lesbians are more subordinated than others. Rogers (1994) points out, for example, that there are more sources of support for young gay men than for lesbians. Those who are members of other subordinated groups may find themselves marginalized both by white, able-bodied lesbian and gay culture, and by their own community (Collins, 1990). Akanke (1994), for example, argues that it is particularly difficult to be out in the black community:

> Within our own Black communities, our sexual preference is seen as a 'white man's disease', inherited from white society/people, which will eventually lead to the demise of the Black race. (p. 103)

Being both black and gay may be made more difficult by racist stereotypes of black masculinity as heterosexually rampant; some white males in particular find it hard to imagine that a black man could be gay at all (Mac an Ghaill, 1994a). At the same time, black lesbians and gay men can be marginalized, as a result of racism, from mainstream lesbian and gay culture:

> Going into the groups, the clubs and the pubs helped me say 'Yes, I'm a lesbian'. But I also became very aware that they were predominantly white, and they didn't take anything into account about being accessible for black people, because they weren't dealing with racism within the groups. So it was like getting into a group and having your identity, but also knowing that within that group they could oppress you. (KOLA: Birmingham Black Lesbian and Gay Group, 1994, pp. 59–60)

Some groups of lesbians, in particular, are not expected to have a sexual life or identity at all. This can make understanding one's own sexuality especially difficult; one is simultaneously conforming to parental expectations and thinking the unthinkable:

> I had a period in India and we were always brought up to think it was terribly wrong to have relationships, full stop. So I knew it would be wrong if I was attracted to girls, from my family's point of view. But I also knew it was wrong to be attracted to boys. (KOLA: Birmingham Black Lesbian and Gay Group, 1994, p. 52)

Appleby (1994) also points out that lesbians with disabilities find themselves marginalized by lesbian groups, which often meet in places with no disabled access, by disabled groups who presume they are heterosexual, and by able-bodied society in general, which assumes they have no sexuality at all. Disabled lesbians and gay men may also find the coming out process particularly difficult if they have no privacy or are dependent on others for obtaining information, for example, about support groups.

Finally, there is one group which is hardly mentioned in the literature about sexual orientation and schooling: the children of lesbians (in most cases) and of gay men. There is little that has been written about this group, but it is clear that homophobic school cultures marginalize these young people in ways similar to those experienced by lesbian and gay teenagers. My own experience (my mother came out when I was fifteen) suggests, as do the few accounts available in the literature (McGuire, 1996; Scott, 1989) that the children of lesbians and gay men have, like lesbians and gay men themselves, to deal with constant need for secrecy and evasion about large areas of their lives, and have similar feelings of fear and relief if and when they come out regarding their home circumstances. Our experiences are also totally absent from the curriculum, even in schools where lesbian and gay teenagers are reasonably well catered for. Those children whose parents are not out to them may also experience feelings of confusion and betrayal, as they gradually come to understand the nature of their parents' relationships (McGuire, 1996).

Summary

This chapter has looked at three groups of people in schools who inhabit subordinated femininities and masculinities. I have argued that the Othering of particular groups of men as non-masculine and the marginalization of women who have a partially masculine physical embodiment is connected to the need, on the part of hegemonic males, to police gender boundaries in the interests of preserving hegemonic male power.

Key Points

- Masculinities and femininities are multiple and contested. Hegemonic masculinity is that which is dominant at a particular time, place and culture.
- Subordinate masculinities are stigmatized as feminine in order to naturalize unequal power relations between different groups of men.
- There are significant disadvantages for those with the option of inhabiting hegemonic masculinities in considering alternatives; this would involve loss of power.
- Sporty girls are often perceived as being outside of the feminine, and therefore challenging. Many adolescent girls reject sports as part of an assertion of femininity.
- Young women athletes are often under pressure to be explicitly feminine and heterosexual.
- Groups of female athletes can, on the other hand, be explicitly supportive of younger sportswomen.
- Homophobia, both in schools and in the wider society, makes life very difficult for lesbians and gay men, and the children of lesbians and gay men, in secondary schools.

Question

In what ways can support for students inhabiting alternative masculinities and femininities be linked to the development of a more female-friendly school culture in general?

Further Reading

CONNELL, R.W. (1995) *Masculinities*, Cambridge: Polity Press, is an excellent interrogation of dominant and subordinated masculinities.

MAC AN GHAILL, M. (1994) *The Making of Men: Masculinities, Sexualities and Schooling*, Buckingham: Open University Press, examines the ways in which different masculinities are fostered and marginalized in secondary schools, based on a detailed study of one school.

EPSTEIN, D. (ed.) (1994) *Challenging Lesbian and Gay Inequalities in Education*, Buckingham: Open University Press, is a selection of writings which consider, from the point of view of both theory and personal experience, what it is like to be gay or lesbian in schools and other educational arenas.

Note

1 Waldner-Haugrud and Magruder (1996) suggest that this may, paradoxically, make the coming out process easier for boys who are already labeled as homosexual because they are not stereotypically masculine. They argue that 'the costs of identity expression are lower for the effeminate gay male who is labeled a homosexual because of his gender nonconformity' (p. 329).

Chapter 9

Strategies: A Toolkit

All my books . . . are, if you like, little tool-boxes. If people want to open them, or to use this sentence or that idea as a screwdriver or spanner to short-circuit, discredit or smash systems of power, including eventually those from which my books have emerged . . . so much the better. (FOUCAULT, M. (1975) Interview with Roger-Pol Droit, *Le Monde*, 21 February 1975, quoted in Patton, 1979, p. 115)

In this book I have considered a number of ways in which girls and young women, along with a number of other groups, are positioned as Other within the education system. The detail in which I have looked at some aspects of this may make it appear as if we were inescapably bound up in an intricate mesh of intersecting power relations, unable to challenge the apparent normality of female oppression. As I argued in Chapter 5, however, it is the very multiplicity of these networks of power which lays them open to challenge; we can, by examining them, find equally multiple points of resistance. The network of micropowers that has allowed men and boys to dominate education can be contested at a number of points.

I argued in Chapter 5 that a key factor in the successful challenge to the Othering of girls and young women within education is detailed knowledge of how this Othering takes place. We need to have clear understandings of what is going on, particularly at the micro level. This allows us both to demonstrate that girls and women are still positioned as Other (despite recent arguments based on girls' improved examination success relative to boys) and to uncover specific weaknesses in the power network, thus making resistance possible. This chapter is intended to help individuals and groups working in schools and similar arenas to map in detail some of the power/ gender networks specific to their situations. Of course, given the space I have, it is neither detailed nor comprehensive, but it should be enough to make a start. The resources cited in the Further Reading section give more detail about specific tools, techniques and activities.

'Traditional' Gender Monitoring

Collating quantitative evidence

'Traditional' gender monitoring in schools has focused largely on the collection and collation of statistics about the relative position of males and females.

Such approaches are somewhat crude, and can mask other, equally important issues. However, they are usually simple to carry out and often use information that the school already has. One can compare, for example, examination entry (numbers and at which level) and success as distributed between boys and girls; it can also be instructive to look at the relative proportions, of those who commence a course, who either take or pass the examination at the end of it. Gender differences regarding choice of subjects, particularly after the end of compulsory education, are also easy to collect and analyse, at least to the extent that large imbalances can be spotted. With younger children, surveys of favourite subjects can themselves be used as mathematics projects, and may even become triggers for discussion of any gender differences that arise.

It is also reasonably easy to compile statistics that compare the formal status of male and female staff. Differences are important here, not only because of the possibly unequal opportunities offered to male and female teachers, but also because young people need to see women (and other marginalized groups) in positions of authority and responsibility. It may also be useful to look at which curriculum and management areas have more female staff, and if it is possible, what they do in that position. Are the heads of science, PE and D&T, for example, male or female, and what are the job titles of their deputies? Is the female deputy head really of equal standing to her two male counterparts, or does she have a vague brief to do with pastoral responsibility for the girls?

Examining curriculum materials

Other, also fairly crude, analyses, can focus on textbooks. Images in texts, for example, can be examined. What is the proportion of males to females shown, and are there differences in what they are shown doing? Do the images of males and females portray them in stereotypical activities and situations, and if not, is this commented on or treated as normal? What sort of examples are used in the text? (Do mathematics problems focus on football scores or the trajectories of cannon-balls; what is the ratio of male to female poets in a collection)? How are particular subjects presented in the books? Do science and mathematics textbooks show a human dimension, or are they presented as detached from the everyday world? Are human values given importance in the design and evaluation of D&T products?

Classroom observation

Another 'traditional' technique is classroom observation. Teachers usually work in pairs, observing each other in the classroom. In any one lesson the focus could be: mapping the teacher's movements around the room and noting how long is spent with boys and girls respectively (and which boys and girls in particular); in whole class lessons or with a small group, recording who gets to speak, and for how long; noting the sorts of questions (open, closed, etc.) the teacher asks of girls or boys, and how long they are given to think before answering. Many studies, some of which have been cited in this book, have found gender differences regarding all of these aspects of classroom life, but it can be helpful to see them at work in one's own context. Useful information about gender relations between students has also been gained from observing boys and girls working together in small groups without the teacher, although such detailed observation is difficult to carry out in one's own classroom.

Examining the Relationship between Space and Power

A number of studies have found a relationship between power relations and the relative space individuals have access to and feel comfortable in (Thorne, 1993; Massey, 1994; Morley, 1992). Examining the use of and dynamics of school spaces can give important clues to the power relations between those inhabiting those spaces.

Classroom plans

The drawing up of classroom plans can give insights into the wider dynamics of the teaching and learning situation. It may be necessary to draw a number of plans, showing seating or working arrangements in different activities or for different teaching groups. Who is near the teacher? Who is in a position to attract the teacher's attention easily? Who is 'where the action is' and who on the periphery? Are any students or groups of students positioned in spaces of maximum invisibility? It may be useful to consider how the seating pattern of a group reflects the internal gender/power relations within that group, as well as the teacher's relationship with individual members.

Staffroom plans

The construction of staffroom power plans can be particularly illuminating of the power/gender relationships between curriculum areas and groups of teachers. Drawing up such a plan can be a trigger for understanding how particular power relations have arisen and are perpetuated in a specific context. For example, in one school I studied, the mathematics department had become permanent squatters on a large proportion of the desk area in the room, despite having departmental office space elsewhere. This reflected the relative power of this department within the school. Alongside the mathematicians sat a male deputy head who had previously been a member and then the head of that department. His residence in the staffroom, as described by another teacher in the school, allowed him to undercut his structurally senior position while, at the same time, making it difficult for

more junior staff, forced to hold meetings in a public place, to challenge his decisions.

> He's got his own beautiful office upstairs here at this end of the school. Beautiful office, computer in it . . . a proper deputy head's office, but he uses two tables here with all his boxes underneath them and he sits in the staffroom. And he does the timetabling there, he does the curriculum there . . . He carries filing cabinet drawers into the staffroom rather than sit in his office to do his work . . . I think he's one of the people who finds it very difficult to get the relationship [right] between being a deputy head and one of the group, one of the staff . . . I feel very angry because . . . if you have a meeting with Paul, it's in that corner with the two tables that you have it. And that really annoys me, because you can't have a proper agenda, really, stuck to, there, especially when there's people listening to you all the time. (Martha Hartwell, Knype School, 10 February 1994)

In other staffrooms, forms of hegemonic masculinity hold sway. One I studied was dominated by a snooker table, used mostly by men, who, by constantly walking around it with their cues, also controlled the surrounding area. In this staffroom the loudest talk was of sporting achievements, and came from a group of men who, while teaching a variety of subjects, allied themselves with the male PE staff and projected a traditionally dominant masculinity constructed around sporting prowess.

The labels teachers give to particular areas of the staffroom also reflect power relations within it. Many schools have a 'supplies' corner' where those staff employed by the day or by the term to cover for absent colleagues are confined in their precarious existence; they are often not fully welcome elsewhere. One staffroom I studied included an area labeled as 'top table'. This was where the disaffected and disenfranchised sat. Some of them were heads of departments, but they did not have the support of a new and very dominant headteacher. Their actual, as opposed to structural power, was very limited, and the label seemed to me to be an assertion of their former status. Another area in this staffroom was known as the 'knitting circle' and was where the feminist teachers sat. In this case the label was used as a put-down for a group that consisted almost entirely of assertive younger women.

Access to virtual space

With the increasing importance of new technology both inside and out of school, access to the 'virtual space' of the Internet and other electronic communications systems will become more relevant to student and teacher progress and life chances. There is already evidence (Spender, 1995) that girls and women use the Internet less than do men and boys, and that they sometimes encounter sexual harassment when doing so. Given that boys also dominate computer clubs at school (Mac an Ghaill, 1994b; Griffiths, 1988), this situation is likely to continue unless teachers and others can persuade girls that electronic communications can benefit them as well as the boys. Schools will need to find ways of monitoring gender variations, among both students and staff, in terms of their confidence, competence and use of the Internet, particularly as a work tool. As has been the case in science education, it may be necessary to explore and emphasize the more human uses of the Net, for example, the support groups for those suffering from particular illnesses, as well as its technological potential. It is also likely to be necessary, as with other uses of computers, to provide female-only sessions to encourage girls. Teachers are also going to need to develop strategies for supporting young women who are harassed in virtual space, so that they do not become permanently alienated from this important medium (Spender, 1995). Virtual space will have to be a particularly important target of all the monitoring and information gathering techniques described in this chapter, if it is not to be colonized by males in the early(ish) stages of its development.

Deconstruction: What-if-Not?

'Deconstruction' is a technical label for the process of asking what appear to be unaskable questions. It involves questioning the assumptions that lie behind beliefs and practices in order to uncover the power relations that are inscribed within them. For example, as I described in Chapter 5, by asking what it would mean for child development not to be a 'natural' process, deconstructionist psychologists were able to undercut a number of gendered assumptions about childrearing, many of which have spilled over into early years education. As I mentioned in Chapter 5, Brown and Walter (1983) call this technique, which they use as a way of getting students to generate and engage with real mathematical problems, 'what-if-not'? They argue that when considering a problem or a situation, we have first to look for the assumptions it contains. We can then ask if these assumptions are correct, and consider how things might be if they were not.

There are a great variety of assumptions to be found in school practices and purposes, and all could benefit from some deconstructive scrutiny. One which has recently been open to challenge has been the idea that it is better to treat subjects as gender-neutral rather than overtly recognizing their gendered nature. This issue has arisen particularly clearly in the cases of holistic D&T and mixed PE. My own research on the former suggests that a move to a supposedly 'neutral' subject could more accurately be described as a partial takeover of 'female' by 'male' subject areas (Paechter, 1993; Paechter and Head, 1996a). The wisdom of mixed PE has been called into question by teachers themselves. They have found that, rather than including girls more within mainstream sport, it has led to their further exclusion, as male games dominate the curriculum, boys refuse to treat girls as full team members and dance has become further marginalized within overall PE provision (Scraton, 1993). Questioning the assumption that mixed groupings will promote equality has resulted in many schools moving back to single-sex classes in this subject.

⚹ Deconstructionist critique can also be approached by making a conscious effort to look at a situation from the point of view of those positioned as Other within it. In the school context, the multiplicity of Others means that there are a number of ways we can approach this. Starting from the position that, to some degree, all children are Other in school, simply tracking one student for a day or a week can give important insights into how school feels for the comparatively powerless. Asking students what they think about particular school subjects can also be illuminating; my own research found, for example, that differences between subjects, from the students' points of view, often centred around things like freedom of movement in the lesson and personal control of some aspects of their learning, rather than on the curriculum content. We can also gain insights from questioning the assumption that lessons are the most important part of the school day. From the students' point of view, it may be what happens in the playground or the dining hall that has most influence on how they feel about school. Given the gendered use of the former area in particular, looking at what goes on in student-dominated arenas is likely to give important insights into the position of Others in school (Thorne, 1993).

Summary

In this chapter I have indicated a number of ways in which the Othering of girls and young women in schools can be investigated at a micro level, and given some suggestions of how such investigations may be approached.

Further Reading

MYERS, K. (ed.) (1992) *Genderwatch: After the Education Reform Act*, Cambridge: Cambridge University Press, contains a wealth of advice and activities for monitoring gender issues in schools, as well as photocopiable sheets designed specifically to support this process.

SALISBURY, J. and JACKSON, D. (1996) *Challenging Macho Values*, London: Falmer Press, is a book specifically for those wanting to work with boys. Suggestions for classroom activities are set alongside the theory that underpins them, making this a valuable resource for teachers.

Chapter 10

Conclusion

We are only trustees for those who come after us. (William Morris, 1877)

The girls and young women in our schools are half our future. Their Othering in this context, combined with their positioning in society as a whole, sets them up for a lifetime of subordination. We can no longer afford the inequity of having half of society functioning as a negative group against which the other half defines itself and asserts its superiority. Furthermore, the current gender regime is detrimental to the other half of our future, boys and young men. While some male groups benefit from the Othering of women, the resulting hegemony of particular forms of masculinity acts against the interests of those who want to take up their maleness in alternative forms. Even for those who benefit from the current regime, it is unhealthy for there to be such a limited range of 'socially acceptable' masculinities. The Othering of the feminine is limiting for both genders. The time for change is long overdue.

Such change has already begun, but has been so threatening to hegemonic masculinity that it has been seen as being at the expense of males. It is significant, for example, that as soon as young women succeeded in moving towards some degree of equity in the outcomes of school leaving examinations, this was interpreted in the popular media as being to the detriment of their male colleagues, and moves were made to amend the examination system once again to favour young men (Weiner et al., 1997). Talk of a 'crisis in masculinity' associated with the loss of traditional male employment in the UK and elsewhere, reflects the persistently strong connections between hegemonic masculine forms and the image of the labouring male as breadwinner. This, however, has not been matched by concern about the continuing inequities in pay and promotional opportunities offered to women, both within and outside of traditional 'female' employment areas. The Othering of women has meant that the loss of 'masculine' jobs and the parallel increase in low-level, 'service' employment traditionally carried out by women has been seen as a triumph for women over men. This discourse overlooks the overwhelming male dominance that remains in the traditional professions and in the higher echelons of the business world.

Schools reflect and at times caricature wider society, particularly in the stereotyped gender role expressions common to adolescence. This means that if we want to tackle the subordination of females in one arena we also need to address it in the other. In both cases, we need to work to challenge and deconstruct the 'normal'; recognize and give value to non-dominant ways of thinking, feeling and expressing; and understand that the long-standing presence of particular ideas and forms of thought in Western philosophy does not mean that these are the only ones that can be useful to us.

Specifically, this means doing a number of things, often in a very small way, to challenge gender/power relations at the micro as well as at the macro level. What today's students learn at school they take out with them into society, so by changing the climate of schools we can affect that society, at least to some degree. We need to work to support challenges, both by teachers and by students, to dominant views of gender, gender roles and sexuality. Those working in primary schools, for example, need overtly to question, as many already do, young children's stereotypical views of what is appropriate behaviour for girls and boys. At the same time, they will have to develop, in conjunction with child psychologists working in this area, a critique of the dominant, masculine-based view of the active developing child. The mantra: 'I do and I understand' (Walkerdine, 1984) needs to be supplemented with equivalent formulations which may be more suited to some children, such as: 'I think about and I understand', 'I ask, what-if-not? and I understand', 'I imitate and I understand', or even, 'I repeat and I understand'. Teachers and others working particularly with adolescents need to find ways of preventing male foreclosure on hegemonic masculine roles, and of protecting from ridicule those, both male and female, who want to take up alternative ways of being. In both these cases, the 'naturalness' of gender polarization, and the associated assumption of heterosexuality, need to be challenged. It is common for young children and adolescents, males in particular, to draw strong boundaries between male and female, but it is not necessarily natural and inevitable. We have to find ways of helping them to see those boundaries as far more blurred and fluid. This will, of course, be difficult. We must accept that, for many males, the breaking down of gender dichotomies results in a loss of the power and privilege of being the Subject to a subordinate Other. Somehow, we have to find ways of helping them to see, and of seeing ourselves, that the sacrifice would amply be repaid by a better, freer and more equitable society for all, including themselves.

Of course it is not sufficient to stop at the school gates. While today's young people will be important in shaping tomorrow's society, they cannot do so alone. It is all very well to educate young women to believe that they have as much potential for career success as their male counterparts, but we have to make this a reality in a society which is at present far from equitable. This means basic, practical things such as providing subsidized childcare to support those women and men who want both to work and to have children, while also fighting against a work culture which prevents them from spending time with those children once they have them. At the same time it means recognizing that women who choose not to have children are neither unnatural nor selfish. It means ensuring that women have access to promotion in all fields and at all levels; this includes finding ways of valuing co-operative work arrangements as well as the masculine, competitive model that still dominates most workplaces. It means making space for voices alternative to those that have dominated Western thought, especially moral thought, since the Enlightenment. Finally, it means recognizing connectedness, as much as independence, both in looking at the ways children develop, and in adult relationships. In short, it means that we must all, both men and women, think and act as feminists.

When a male baby comes to the realization that his mother is not of himself, but is a separate being, he sees her simply as different, not as inferior. To say that I am like this and not like that does not have to render subordinate that which I am not. In asking for a world in which we are all Subjects, I am not asking for the elimination of difference. I am, rather, asking that we deconstruct, demolish and de-naturalize the power relation that currently exists between Subject and Other.

Bibliography

AKANKE (1994) 'Black in the closet', in EPSTEIN, D. (ed.) *Challenging Lesbian and Gay Inequalities in Education*, Buckingham: Open University Press, pp. 101–13.

ANG-LYGATE, M. (1996) 'Waking from a dream of Chinese shadows', *Feminism and Psychology*, **6**, 1, pp. 56–60.

APPLEBY, Y. (1994) 'Out in the margins', *Disability and Society*, **9**, 1, pp. 19–32.

ARCHER, J. (1992) 'Gender stereotyping of school subjects', *The Psychologist: Bulletin of the British Psychological Society*, **5**, pp. 66–9.

ARNOT, M., DAVID, M. and WEINER, G. (1996) *Educational Reform and Gender Equality in Schools*, Manchester: Equal Opportunities Commission.

ASKEW, S. and Ross, C. (1988) *Boys Don't Cry: Boys and Sexism in Education*, Milton Keynes: Open University Press.

ATTAR, D. (1990) *Wasting Girls' Time: The History and Politics of Home Economics*, London: Virago Press.

AZIZ, R. (1997) 'Feminism and the challenge of racism: Deviance or difference?', in MIRZA, H.S. (ed.) *Black British Feminism*, London: Routledge, pp. 70–7.

BACK, L. (1994) 'The "White Negro" revisited: Race and masculinities in South London', in CORNWALL, A. and LINDISFARNE, N. (eds.) *Dislocating Masculinity*, London: Routledge, pp. 172–83.

BEM, S.L. (1993) *The Lenses of Gender: Transforming the Debate on Sexual Inequality*, New Haven: Yale University Press.

BERGER, J. (1972) *Ways of Seeing*, London: BBC and Penguin Books.

BLACK, E. (1989) 'Women's work in a man's world: Secretarial training in a College of Further Education', in ACKER, S. (ed.) *Teachers, Gender and Careers*, Lewes: Falmer Press, pp. 139–50.

BLOOT, R. and BROWNE, J. (1996) 'Reasons for the underrepresentation of females at head of department level in physical education in government schools in Western Australia', *Gender and Education*, **8**, 1, pp. 81–101.

BOALER, J. (1997) Mathematical equity — Under achieving boys or sacrificial girls? Paper presented at the ESRC seminar series, *Gender and Education: Are Boys Now Underachieving?*, Institute of Education, London.

BOLDT, G.M. (1996) 'Sexist and heterosexist responses to gender bending in an elementary classroom', *Curriculum Inquiry*, **26**, 2, pp. 113–31.

BRITTAN, A. (1989) *Masculinity and Power*, Oxford: Basil Blackwell.

BROWN, L.M. and GILLIGAN, C. (1993) 'Meeting at the crossroads: Women's psychology and girls' development', *Feminism and Psychology*, **3**, 1, pp. 11–35.

BROWN, S.I. (1986) 'The logic of problem generation: From morality and solving to de-posing and rebellion', in BURTON, L. (ed.) *Girls into Maths Can Go*, Eastbourne: Holt, Rinehart and Winston, pp. 196–222.

BROWN, S.I. and WALTER, M. (1983) *The Art of Problem Posing*, New Jersey: Lawrence Erlbaum Associates.

BROWNMILLER, S. (1984) *Femininity*, London: Paladin.

BRYSON, L. (1987) 'Sport and the maintenance of masculine hegemony', *Women's Studies International Forum*, **10**, 4, pp. 349–60.

BUCHBINDER, D. (1994) *Masculinities and Identities*, Melbourne: Melbourne University Press.

BURCHELL, H. (1995) 'Gender and records of achievement', *Pastoral Care in Education*, **13**, 1, pp. 8–11.

BURMAN, E. (1994) *Deconstructing Developmental Psychology*, London: Routledge.

BURMAN, E. (1995) '"What is it?" Masculinity and femininity in cultural representations of childhood', in WILKINSON, S. and KITZINGER, C. (eds.) *Feminism and Discourse*, London: Sage, pp. 49–67.

BURTON, L. (1989) 'Images of mathematics', in ERNEST, P. (ed.) *Mathematics Teaching: The State of the Art*, Lewes: Falmer Press, pp. 180–7.

BURTON-NELSON, M. (1994–5) 'Unfair play', *Trouble and Strife*, **29/30**, pp. 14–21.

BUTLER, J. (1990) *Gender Trouble: Feminism and the Subversion of Identity*, London: Routledge.

CAMERON, D. (1995) 'Rethinking language and gender studies: Some issues for the 1990s', in MILLS, S. (ed.) *Language and Gender: Interdisciplinary Perspectives*, Harlow, Essex: Longman, pp. 31–44.

CARBY, H.V. (1997) 'White woman listen! Black feminism and the boundaries of sisterhood', in MIRZA, H.S. (ed.) *Black British Feminism*, London: Routledge, pp. 45–53.

CARRIGAN, T., CONNELL, B. and LEE, J. (1985) 'Toward a new sociology of masculinity', *Theory and Society*, **14**, pp. 551–604.

CARRINGTON, B. and WOOD, E. (1983) 'Body talk: Images of sport in a multi-racial school', *Multiracial Education*, **11**, 2, pp. 29–38.

CARROLL, B. (1986) '"Troublemakers": Making a name in physical education', in EVANS, J. (ed.) *Physical Education, Sport and Schooling*, Lewes: Falmer Press, pp. 117–32.

CARROLL, B. (1995) Gender and other factors influencing the choice of examination subjects. Paper presented at European Conference on Educational Research, Bath, September 1995.

CARROLL, B. and HOLLINSHEAD, G. (1993) 'Ethnicity and conflict in physical education', *British Educational Research Journal*, **19**, 1, pp. 59–76.

CHODOROW, N. (1978) *The Reproduction of Mothering: Psychoanalysis and the Sociology of Gender*, Berkeley: University of California Press.

CHODOROW, N.J. (1995) 'Gender as a personal and social construction', *Signs*, **20**, 3, pp. 516–44.

COATES, J. (1994) 'No gap, lots of overlap: Turn-taking patterns in the talk of women friends', in GRADDOL, D., MAYBIN, J. and STIERER, B. (eds.) *Researching Language and Literacy in Social Context*, Clevedon: Multilingual Matters Ltd, pp. 177–92.

COLES, F. (1994–5) 'Feminine charms and outrageous arms', *Trouble and Strife*, **29/30**, pp. 67–72.

COLLINS, P.H. (1990) *Black Feminist Thought*, London: Unwin Hyman.

CONNELL, R.W. (1987) *Gender and Power*, Cambridge: Polity Press.

CONNELL, R.W. (1994) 'The state, gender and sexual politics: Theory and appraisal', in RADTKE, H.L. and STAM, H.J. (eds.) *Power/Gender*, London: Sage, pp. 136–73.

CONNELL, R.W. (1995) *Masculinities*, Cambridge: Polity Press.

CONNELL, R.W., ASHENDEN, D.J., KESSLER, S. and DOWSETT, G.W. (1982) *Making the Difference: Schools, Families and Social Division*, London: Allen and Unwin.

COYLE, A. (1996) 'Representing men with HIV/AIDS', *Feminism and Psychology*, **6**, 1, pp. 79–85.

CROZIER, J. and ANSTISS, J. (1995) 'Out of the spotlight: Girls' experience of disruption', in LLOYD-SMITH, M. and DWYFOR DAVIES, J. (eds.) *On the Margins: The Educational Experience of 'Problem' Pupils*, Stoke-on-Trent: Trentham Books, pp. 30–47.

CUNNISON, S. (1989) 'Gender joking in the staffroom', in ACKER, S. (ed.) *Teachers, Gender and Careers*, Lewes: Falmer Press, pp. 151–67.

DAVIES, B. (1989) 'The discursive production of the male/female dualism in school settings', *Oxford Review of Education*, **15**, 3, pp. 229–41.

DAVIN, A. (1987) ' "Mind that you do as you are told": Reading books for Board School girls, 1870–1902', in ARNOT, M. and WEINER, G. (eds.) *Gender Under Scrutiny*, London: Hutchinson, pp. 143–49.

DE BEAUVOIR, S. (1949) *The Second Sex*, Harmondsworth, Middlesex: Penguin Books.

DeFRANCISCO, V. (1992) 'Deborah Tannen: You just don't understand: Women and men in conversation', *Language in Society*, **21**, 2, pp. 319–23.

DELAMONT, S. (1994) 'Accentuating the positive: Refocusing the research on girls and science', *Studies in Science Education*, **23**, pp. 59–74.

DEPARTMENT FOR EDUCATION AND EMPLOYMENT (1996) *Statistics of Education: Public Examinations in GCSE and GCE in England 1995*, London: HMSO.

DERRIDA, J. (1974) *Of Grammatology*, Baltimore: John Hopkins University Press.

DEWAR, A. (1990) 'Oppression and privilege in physical education: Struggles in the negotiation of gender in a university programme', in KIRK, D. and TINNING, R. (eds.) *Physical Education, Curriculum and Culture*, Basingstoke: Falmer Press, pp. 67–99.

DI STEFANO, C. (1990) 'Dilemmas of difference: Feminism, modernity and postmodernism', in NICHOLSON, L.J. (ed.) *Feminism/Postmodernism*, London: Routledge, pp. 63–82.

DIAMOND, M. and SIGMUNDSON, K. (1997) 'Sex reassignment at birth: Long-term review and clinical implications', *Archives of Pediatric Adolescent Medicine*, **151**, pp. 298–304.

DIXON, C. (1997) 'Pete's tool: Identity and sex-play in the design and technology classroom', *Gender and Education*, **9**, 1, pp. 89–104.

DONALDSON, M. (1993) 'What is hegemonic masculinity?', *Theory and Society*, **22**, pp. 643–57.

DRAPER, J. (1991) Encounters with sex and gender: some issues arising out of the transition from a single sex to a mixed school. Paper presented at St Hilda's Conference on Education and Qualitative Research: Teaching, Learning and Educational Change, University of Warwick, September 1991.

DUNCAN, J. (1993) 'Place, time and the discourse of the Other', in DUNCAN, J. and LEY, D. (eds.) *Place, Culture and Representation*, London: Routledge, pp. 39–56.

DYHOUSE, C. (1976) 'Social Darwinistic ideas and the development of women's education 1880–1920', *History of Education*, **5**, 1, pp. 41–58.

DYHOUSE, C. (1977) 'Good wives and little mothers: Social anxieties and the schoolgirl's curriculum 1890–1920', *Oxford Review of Education*, **3**, 1, pp. 21–35.

DYHOUSE, C. (1978) 'Towards a "feminine" curriculum for English schoolgirls: The demands of ideology 1870–1963', *Womens' Studies International Quarterly*, **1**, pp. 291–311.

ELLSWORTH, E. (1989) 'Why doesn't this feel empowering? Working through the myths of critical pedagogy', *Harvard Educational Review*, **59**, 3, pp. 297–324.

EPSTEIN, D. and JOHNSON, R. (1994) 'On the straight and narrow: The heterosexual presumption, homophobias and schools', in EPSTEIN, D. (ed.) *Challenging Lesbian and Gay Inequalities in Education*, Buckingham: Open University Press, pp. 197–230.

FASTING, K. (1987) 'Sports and women's culture', *Women's Studies International Forum*, **10**, 4, pp. 361–68.

FAUSTO-STERLING, A. (1987) 'Society writes biology/biology constructs gender', *Daedalus*, **116**, pp. 61–76.

FAUSTO-STERLING, A. (1989) 'Life in the XY corral', *Women's Studies International Forum*, **12**, 3, pp. 319–31.

FISHER, J. (1994) 'Unequal races: Gender and assessment', in GRADDOL, D., MAYBIN, J. and STIERER, B. (eds.) *Researching Language and Literacy in Social Context*, Clevedon: Multilingual Matters Ltd, pp. 168–76.

FITZCLARENCE, L. and GIROUX, H. (1984) 'The paradox of power in educational theory and practice', *Language Arts*, **61**, 5, pp. 462–77.

FLAX, J. (1990) 'Postmodernism and gender relations in feminist theory', in NICHOLSON, L.J. (ed.) *Feminism/Postmodernism*, London: Routledge, pp. 39–62.

FLETCHER, S. (1984) *Women First*, London: The Althone Press.

FLINTOFF, A. (1993) 'Gender, physical education and initial teacher education', in EVANS, J. (ed.) *Equality, Education and Physical Education*, London: Falmer Press, pp. 184–204.

FORDHAM, S. (1996) *Blacked Out: Dilemmas of Race, Identity and Success at Captial High*, Chicago: University of Chicago Press.

FOUCAULT, M. (1963) *The Birth of the Clinic*, London: Routledge.

FOUCAULT, M. (1977) *Discipline and Punish*, London: Penguin.

FOUCAULT, M. (1978) *The History of Sexuality Volume One*, London: Penguin.

FOUCAULT, M. (1979) 'Power and norm: Notes', in MORRIS, M. and PATTON, P. (eds.) *Michel Foucault, Power, Truth, Strategy*, Sydney: Feral Publications, pp. 59–66.

FOUCAULT, M. (1980) *Power/Knowledge: Selected Interviews and Other Writings 1972–1977*, Hemel Hempstead, Herts: Harvester Press.

FOUCAULT, M. (1982) 'The subject and power', in DREYFUS, H.L. and RABINOV, P. (eds.) *Michel Foucault: Beyond Structuralism and Hermeneutics*, Brighton: Harvester Press, pp. 208–26.

FOUCAULT, M. (1988) *Politics, Philosophy, Culture: Interviews and Other Writings 1977–1984*, London: Routledge.

FRANCIS, B. (1997) 'Power plays: Children's construction of gender and power in role plays', *Gender and Education*, **9**, 2, pp. 179–91.

FREIRE, P. (1972) *Pedagogy of the Oppressed*, Middlesex: Penguin.

FRENCH, M. (1994) 'Power/sex', in RADTKE, H.L. and STAM, H.J. (eds.) *Power/Gender*, London: Sage, pp. 15–35.

GATENS, M. (1991) *Feminism and Philosophy: Perspectives on Difference and Equality*, Cambridge: Polity Press.

GILLBORN, D. (1990) *'Race', Ethnicity and Education*, London: Unwin Hyman.

GILLIGAN, C. (1982) *In a Different Voice: Psychological Theory and Women's Development*, Cambridge, Mass: Harvard University Press.

GILLIGAN, C. and ATTANUCCI, J. (1988) 'Two moral orientations: Gender differences and similarities', *Merrill-Palmer Quarterly*, **34**, 3, pp. 223–37.

GIPPS, C. and MURPHY, P. (1994) *A Fair Test? Assessment, Achievement and Equity*, Buckingham: Open University Press.

GIROUX, H.A. (1981) *Ideology, Culture and the Politics of Schooling*, London: Falmer Press.

GIROUX, H.A. (1988a) 'Critical theory and the politics of culture and voice: Rethinking the discourse of educational research', in SHERMANN, R.R. and WEBB, R.B. (eds.) *Qualitative Research in Education: Focus and Methods*, Lewes: Falmer Press, pp. 190–210.

GIROUX, H.A. (1988b) 'Postmodernism and the discourse of educational criticism', *Journal of Education*, **170**, 3, pp. 5–30.

GIROUX, H.A. (1988c) *Schooling for Democracy*, London: Routledge.

GRAMSCI, A. (1971) *Selections from the Prison Notebooks of Antonio Gramsci*, London: Lawrence and Wishart.

GREENO, C.G. and MACCOBY, E.E. (1986) 'How different is the different voice?' *Signs*, **11**, 2, pp. 310–16.

GRIFFIN, P. (1991) 'Identity management strategies among lesbian and gay educators', *Qualitative Studies in Education*, **4**, 3, pp. 189–202.

GRIFFIN, P. (1992) 'Changing the game: Homophobia, sexism and lesbians in sport', *Quest*, **44**, pp. 251–65.

GRIFFITHS, M. (1988) 'Strong feelings about computers', *Women's Studies International Forum*, **11**, 2, pp. 145–54.

HARBSMEIER, M. (1985) 'On travel accounts and cosmological strategies: Some models in comparative xenology', *Ethnos*, **50**, pp. 273–312.

HEAD, J.O. (1997) *Working with Adolescents: Constructing Identity*, London: Falmer Press.

HEARN, J. (1996) 'Is masculinity dead? A critique of the concept of masculinity/masculinities', in MAC AN GHAILL, M. (ed.) *Understanding Masculinities: Social Relations and Cultural Arenas*, Buckingham: Open University Press, pp. 202–17.

HECKMAN, S.J. (1990) *Gender and Knowledge: Elements of a Postmodern Feminism*, Cambridge: Polity Press.

HEKMAN, S.J. (1995) *Moral Voices, Moral Selves: Carol Gilligan and Feminist Moral Theory*, Cambridge: Polity Press.

HOLLOWAY, W. (1984) 'Gender difference and the production of subjectivity', in HENRIQUES, J., HOLLOWAY, W., URWIN, C., VENN, C. and WALKERDINE, V. (eds.) *Changing the Subject*, London: Methuen, pp. 227–63.

hooks, b. (1982) *Ain't I a Woman: Black Women and Feminism*, London: Pluto Press.

HOSKIN, K. (1990) 'Foucault under examination: The crypto-educationalist revealed', in BALL, S.J. (ed.) *Foucault and Education*, London: Routledge, pp. 29–53.

HUMBERSTONE, B. (1993) 'Equality, physical education and outdoor education — ideological struggles and transformative structures?' in EVANS, J. (ed.) *Equality, Education and Physical Education*, London: Falmer Press, pp. 217–32.

HUNT, F. (1987) 'Divided aims: The educational implications of opposing ideologies in girls' secondary schooling 1850–1940', in HUNT, F. (ed.) *Lessons for Life*, Oxford: Basil Blackwell, pp. 3–21.

IMPERATO-MCGINLEY, J., PETERSON, R.E., GAUTIER, T. and STURIA, E. (1979) 'Androgens and the evolution of male gender-identity among male pseudohermaphrodites with 5-alpha reductase deficiency', *New England Journal of Medicine*, **300**, pp. 1233–37.

INNER LONDON EDUCATION AUTHORITY (1984) *Providing Equal Opportunities for Girls and Boys in Physical Education*, London: Inner London Education Authority.

JIPSON, J., MUNRO, P., VICTOR, S., FROUDE JONES, K. and FREED-ROWLAND, G. (1995) *Repositioning Feminism and Education: Perspectives on Educating for Social Change*, Westport, Connecticut/London: Bergin and Garvey.

JOHNSON, S. and MURPHY, P. (1986) *Girls and Physics*, London: Department of Education and Science.

JOHNSTON, L. (1996) 'Flexing femininity: Female body-builders refiguring "the body"', *Gender, Place and Culture*, **3**, 3, pp. 327–40.

JONES, A. and KIRK, C.M. (1990) 'Gender differences in students' interests in applications of school physics', *Physics Education*, **25**, pp. 308–13.

KEELY, P. and MYERS, K. (1983) 'Business studies', in WHYLD, J. (ed.) *Sexism in the Secondary Curriculum*, London: Harper and Row, pp. 237–47.

KENWAY, J. (1996) 'Reasserting masculinity in Australian schools', *Women's Studies International Forum*, **19**, 4, pp. 447–66.

KESSLER, S. and MCKENNA, W. (1978) *Gender: An Ethnomethodological Approach*, New York: John Wiley and Sons.

KESSLER, S.J. (1990) 'The medical construction of gender: Case management of intersexed infants', *Signs*, **16**, 1, pp. 3–26.

KESSLER, S., ASHENDEN, D.J., CONNELL, R.W. and DOWSETT, G.W. (1985) 'Gender relations in secondary schooling', *Sociology of Education*, **58**, pp. 34–48.

KIMURA, D. (1992) 'Sex differences in the brain', *Scientific American*, September, pp. 81–7.

KITZINGER, C. (1987) *The Social Construction of Lesbianism*, London: Sage Publications.

KITZINGER, C. (1994a) 'Listening to a different voice', *Feminism and Psychology*, **4**, 3, pp. 408–19.

KITZINGER, C. (1994b) 'Listening with mothers', *Times Higher Education Supplement*, London, 4 March, p. 17.

KLEINER, K. (1996) 'Testing the gender gap', *New Scientist*, **152**, 2055, 23 November, p. 49.

KOLA: BIRMINGHAM BLACK LESBIAN AND GAY GROUP (1994) 'A burden of aloneness', in EPSTEIN, D. (ed.) *Challenging Lesbian and Gay Inequalities in Education*, Buckingham: Open University Press, pp. 49–64.

KRAMARAE, C. (1992) 'Speaking freely: Unlearning the lies of our father's tongues; You just don't understand: Women and men in conversation; Telling it: Women and language across cultures', *Signs*, **17**, 3, pp. 666–71.

LANDAU, N.R. (1994) 'Love, hate and mathematics', MA. Dissertation, King's College, London.

LATHER, P. (1991) *Getting Smart*, London: Routledge.

LEAMAN, O. (1984) *'Sit on the Sidelines and Watch the Boys Play': Sex Differentiation in Physical Education*, York: Longman.

LEE, V.E., CRONINGER, R.G., LINN, E. and CHEN, X. (1996) 'The culture of sexual harassment in secondary schools', *American Educational Research Journal*, **33**, 2, pp. 383–417.

LEES, S. (1993) *Sugar and Spice: Sexuality and Adolescent Girls*, London: Penguin Books.

LENSKYJ, J. (1987) 'Female sexuality and women's sport', *Women's Studies International Forum*, **10**, 4, pp. 381–6.

LEWIS, M. (1990) 'Interrupting patriarchy: Politics, resistance and transformation in the femininst classroom', *Harvard Educational Review*, **60**, 4, pp. 467–88.

LIGHTFOOT, S.L. (1986) 'On goodness in schools: Themes of empowerment', *Peabody Journal of Education*, **63**, 3, pp. 9–26.

LLOYD, B. and DUVEEN, G. (1992) *Gender Identities and Education: The Impact of Starting School*, Hemel Hempstead, Herts: Harvester Press.

LOBEL, T.E. and MENSHARI, J. (1993) 'Relations of conceptions of gender-role transgressions and gender constancy to gender-typed toy preferences', *Developmental Psychology*, **29**, 1, pp. 150–5.

LUKE, C. (1994) 'Women in the academy: The politics of speech and silence', *British Journal of Sociology of Education*, **15**, 2, pp. 211–30.

LUKES, S. (1974) *Power: A Radical View*, Basingstoke: Macmillan.

MAC AN GHAILL, M. (1994a) '(In)visibility, sexuality, race and masculinity in the school context', in EPSTEIN, D. (ed.) *Challenging Lesbian and Gay Inequalities in Education*, Buckingham: Open University Press, pp. 152–76.

MAC AN GHAILL, M. (1994b) *The Making of Men: Masculinities, Sexualities and Schooling*, Buckingham: Open University Press.

MAC AN GHAILL, M. (1996) 'Deconstructing heterosexualities within school arenas', *Curriculum Studies*, **4**, 2, pp. 191–209.

MANTHORPE, C. (1986) Science or domestic science? The struggle to define an appropriate science education for girls in early twentieth-century England', *History of Education*, **15**, 3, pp. 195–213.

MANTHORPE, C. (1989) 'Reflections on the scientific education of girls', in MOON, B., MURPHY, P. and RAYNOR, J. (eds.) *Policies for the Curriculum*, London: Hodder and Stoughton, pp. 119–30.

MARTIN, C.L. and LITTLE, J.K. (1990) 'The relation of gender understanding to children's sex-typed preferences and gender stereotypes', *Child Development*, **61**, pp. 1427–39.

MASSEY, D. (1994) *Space, Place and Gender*, Cambridge: Polity Press.

MASSEY, D. (1995) 'Masculinity, dualisms and high technology', *Transactions of the Institute of British Geographers*, **20**, 4, pp. 487–99.

McGUIRE, M. (1996) 'Livin' in a gay family', *Harvard Educational Review*, **66**, 2, pp. 182–84.

McLEOD, J., YATES, L. and HALASA, K. (1993) Voice, difference and feminist pedagogy. Paper presented at British Educational Research Association Annual Conference, University of Liverpool, September 1993.

McNAY, L. (1992) *Foucault and Feminism*, Cambridge: Polity Press.

McROBBIE, A. (1991) *Feminism and Youth Culture*, Basingstoke: Macmillan Education.

MELIA, J. (1996) Keeping quiet in class: Researching lesbian teachers. Paper presented at British Educational Research Association Annual Conference, Lancaster University, September 1996.

MILLS, M. (1996) ' "Homophobia kills": A disruptive moment in the educational politics of legitimation', *British Journal of Sociology of Education*, **17**, 3, pp. 315–26.

MIRZA, H.S. (1997) 'Black women in education: A collective movement for social change', in MIRZA, H.S. (ed.) *Black British Feminism*, London: Routledge, pp. 269–77.

MONEY, J. and EHRHARDT, A.A. (1972) *Man and Woman Boy and Girl: The Differentiation and Dimorphism of Gender Identity from Conception to Maturity*, Baltimore: Johns Hopkins University Press.

MORGAN, E. (1972) *The Descent of Woman*, London: Corgi Books.

MORLEY, D. (1992) *Television Audiences and Cultural Studies*, London: Routledge.

MORSS, J. (1996) *Growing Critical: Alternatives to Developmental Psychology*, London: Routledge.

MURPHY, P.F. (1990) Gender difference: Implications for assessment and curriculum planning. Paper presented at British Educational Research Association, Roehampton Institute, London, September 1990.

MURPHY, P. and ELWOOD, J. (1997) Gendered experiences, choices and achievement — Exploring the links. Paper presented at Equity Issues in Gender and Assessment. 23rd Annual Conference of the International Association for Educational Assessment, Durban, South Africa, June 1997.

MYERS, D.J. and DUGAN, K.B. (1996) 'Sexism in graduate school classrooms: Consequences for students and faculty', *Gender and Society*, **10**, 3, pp. 330–50.

NICHOLSON, L. (1994) 'Interpreting gender', *Signs*, **20**, 1, pp. 79–105.

OHRN, E. (1993) 'Gender, influence and resistance in school', *British Journal of Sociology of Education*, **14**, 2, pp. 147–58.

ORBACH, S. (1993) 'Heterosexuality and parenting', in WILKINSON, S. and KITZINGER, C. (eds.) *Heterosexuality: A Feminism and Psychology Reader*, London: Sage, pp. 48–9.

OSBORNE, J. (1990) 'Sacred cows of physics — Towards a redefinition of physics education', *Physics Education*, **25**, pp. 189–95.

PAECHTER, C.F. (1993) 'What happens when a school subject undergoes a sudden change of status?' *Curriculum Studies*, **1**, 3, pp. 349–64.

PAECHTER, C.F. and HEAD, J.O. (1995) Power and gender influences on curriculum implementation. Paper presented at American Educational Research Association Annual Meeting, San Francisco, April 1995.

PAECHTER, C.F. and HEAD, J.O. (1996a) 'Gender, identity, status and the body: Life in a marginal subject', *Gender and Education*, **8**, 1, pp. 21–30.

PAECHTER, C.F. and HEAD, J.O. (1996b) 'Power and gender in the staffroom', *British Educational Research Journal*, **22**, 1, pp. 57–69.

PARKER, A. (1996a) 'Sporting masculinities: Gender relations and the body', in MAC AN GHAILL, M. (ed.) *Understanding Masculinities: Social Relations and Cultural Arenas*, Buckingham: Open University Press, pp. 126–38.

PARKER, A. (1996b) 'The construction of masculinity within boys' physical education', *Gender and Education*, **8**, 2, pp. 141–57.

PATTON, P. (1979) 'Of power and prisons', in MORRIS, M. and PATTON, P. (eds.) *Michel Foucault, Power, Truth, Strategy*, Sydney: Feral Publications, pp. 109–47.

PENFOLD, J. (1988) *Craft, Design and Technology: Past, Present and Future*, Stoke on Trent: Trentham Books.

PETERS, R.S. (1965) 'Education as initiation', in ARCHAMBAULT, R.D. (ed.) *Philosophical Analysis and Education*, London: Routledge and Kegan Paul, pp. 87–112.

POLLOCK, G. (1988) *Vision and Difference: Femininity, Feminism and the Histories of Art*, London: Routledge.

PORTER, P. (1991) 'The state-family-workplace intersection: Hegemony, contradictions and counter-hegemony in education', in DAWKINS, D. (ed.) *Power and Politics in Education*, London: Falmer Press, pp. 9–52.

POTTS, P. (1996) Progress and reproduction: Gender and membership of the mainstream. Paper presented at Critical Issues on Inclusion and Exclusion: A national seminar series, Open University, Milton Keynes, March 1996.

PRYOR, J. (1993) He, she and IT: Groupwork in a gender-sensitive area. Paper presented at British Educational Research Association Annual Conference, University of Liverpool, September 1993.

PURVIS, J. (1985) 'Domestic subjects since 1870', in GOODSON, I.F. (ed.) *Social Histories of the Secondary Curriculum*, Lewes: Falmer Press, pp. 145–76.

PYKE, K.D. (1996) 'Class-based masculinities: The interdependence of gender, class and interpersonal power', *Gender and Society*, **10**, 5, pp. 527–49.

RANDALL, G.J. (1987) 'Gender differences in pupil-teacher interaction in workshops and laboratories', in ARNOT, M. and WEINER, G. (eds.) *Gender Under Scrutiny*, London: Hutchinson, pp. 163–72.

RAWLS, J. (1972) *A Theory of Justice*, Oxford: Oxford University Press.

REDMAN, P. (1996) 'Empowering men to disempower themselves: Heterosexual masculinities, HIV and the contradictions of anti-oppressive education', in MAC AN GHAILL, M. (ed.) *Understanding Masculinities: Social Relations and Cultural Arenas*, Buckingham: Open University Press, pp. 168–79.

REDMAN, P. (1997) Educating Peter: Schooling, the unconscious and the production of heterosexual masculinities. Paper presented at Transitions in Gender and Education, University of Warwick, April 1997.

RENSENBRINK, C.W. (1996) 'What difference does it make? The story of a lesbian teacher', *Harvard Educational Review*, **66**, 2, pp. 257–70.

RICH, A. (1980) 'Compulsory heterosexuality and lesbian existence', *Signs*, **5**, 4, pp. 631–60.

RICHARDSON, D. (ed.) (1996) *Theorising Heterosexuality*, Buckingham: Open University Press, 1996.

RIDDELL, S. (1990) Pupils, resistance and gender codes: A study of classroom encounters, *Gender and Education*, **1**, 2, pp. 183–97.

RIDDELL, S. (1992) *Gender and the Politics of the Curriculum*, London: Routledge.

ROBINSON, K.H. (1992) 'Class-room discipline: Power, resistance and gender. A look at teacher perspectives', *Gender and Education*, **4**, 3, pp. 273–87.

ROGERS, C. (1983) *Freedom to Learn for the 80s*, Columbus, Ohio: Charles E. Merrill.

ROGERS, M. (1994) 'Growing up lesbian: The role of the school', in EPSTEIN, D. (ed.) *Challenging Lesbian and Gay Inequalities in Education*, Buckingham: Open University Press, pp. 31–48.

ROUSSEAU, J.-J. (1979) *Emile*, London: Penguin.

SACKS, O. (1993) 'Making up the mind', *New York Review of Books*, 8 April, New York: pp. 42–7.

SAID, E.W. (1978) *Orientalism*, London: Penguin.

SALISBURY, J. and JACKSON, D. (1996) *Challenging Macho Values: Practical Ways of Working with Adolescent Boys*, London: Falmer Press.

SANDERS, S.A.L. and BURKE, H. (1994) 'Are you a lesbian, miss?' in EPSTEIN, D. (ed.) *Challenging Lesbian and Gay Inequalities in Education*, Buckingham: Open University Press, pp. 65–77.

SCHUTZ, A. (1964) 'The stranger', in COSIN, B.R., DALE, I.R., ESLAND, G.M., MACKINNON, D. and SWIFT, D.F. (eds.) *School and Society*, London: Routledge and Kegan Paul, pp. 27–33.

SCOTT, P. (1989) 'Challenging heterosexism in the classroom: Roles for teachers, governors and parents', in JONES, C. and MAHONY, P. (eds.) *Learning Our Lines: Sexuality and Social Control in Education*, London: The Women's Press, pp. 249–77.

SCRATON, S. (1986) 'Images of femininity and the teaching of girls' physical education', in EVANS, J. (ed.) *Physical Education, Sport and Schooling*, Lewes: Falmer Press, pp. 71–94.

SCRATON, S. (1993) 'Equality, coeducation and physical education', in EVANS, J. (ed.) *Equality, Education and Physical Education*, London: Falmer Press, pp. 139–53.

SHERLOCK, J. (1987) 'Issues of masculinity and femininity in British physical education', *Women's Studies International Forum*, **10**, 4, pp. 443–51.

SHILLING, C. (1991) 'Social space, gender inequalities and educational differentiation', *British Journal of Sociology of Education*, **12**, 1, pp. 23–44.

SHILLING, C. (1992) 'Schooling and the production of physical capital', *Discourse*, **13**, 1, pp. 1–19.

SHILLING, C. (1993) *The Body and Social Theory*, London: Sage Publications.

SIKES, P.J. (1988) 'Growing old gracefully? Age, identity and physical education', in EVANS, J. (ed.) *Teachers, Teaching and Control in Physical Education*, Lewes: Falmer Press, pp. 21–40.

SIRAJ-BLATCHFORD, I. (1993) 'Ethnicity and conflict in physical education: A critique of Carroll and Hollinshead's study', *British Educational Research Journal*, **19**, 1, pp. 77–82.

SMART, B. (1986) 'The politics of truth and the problem of hegemony', in COUZENS HOY, D. (ed.) *Foucault, A Critical Reader*, Oxford: Basil Blackwell, pp. 149–55.

SMITH, C. and LLOYD, B. (1978) 'Maternal behavior and perceived sex of infant: Revisited', *Child Development*, **49**, pp. 1263–5.

SMITH, D.E. (1990) *The Conceptual Practices of Power*, Boston: NE University Press.

SPARKES, A., TEMPLIN, T.J. and SCHEMPP, P.G. (1990) 'The problematic nature of a career in a marginal subject: Some implications for teacher education', *Journal of Education for Teaching*, **16**, 1, pp. 3–28.

SPARKES, A.C. (1991a) 'Alternative visions of health-related fitness: An exploration of problem-setting and its consequences', in ARMSTRONG, N. and SPARKES, A. (eds.) *Issues in Physical Education*, London: Cassell, pp. 204–27.

SPARKES, A.C. (1991b) 'Exploring the subjective dimension of curriculum change', in ARMSTRONG, N. and SPARKES, A. (eds.) *Issues in Physical Education*, London: Cassell, pp. 20–35.

SPARKES, A.C. (1994) 'Self, silence and invisibility as a beginning teacher: A life history of lesbian experience', *British Journal of Sociology of Education*, **15**, 1, pp. 93–118.

SPELMAN, E.V. (1982) 'Woman as body: Ancient and contemporary views', *Feminist Studies*, **8**, 1, pp. 109–31.

SPENDER, D. (1982) *Invisible Women: The Schooling Scandal*, London: Writers and Readers Publishing Cooperative.

SPENDER, D. (1995) *Nattering on the Net*, Melbourne: Spinfex Pty Ltd.

STABLES, A. (1990) 'Differences between pupils from mixed and single-sex schools in their enjoyment of school subjects and in their attitudes to science and to school', *Educational Review*, **42**, 3, pp. 221–30.

STABLES, A. and WIKELEY, F. (1996) Pupil approaches to subject option choices. Paper presented at European Educational Research Association Conference, Seville, October.

STACK, C.B. (1986) 'The culture of gender: Women and men of color', *Signs*, **11**, 2, pp. 321–4.

SULLIVAN, C. (1993) 'Oppression: The experiences of a lesbian teacher in an inner city comprehensive school in the United Kingdom', *Gender and Education*, **5**, 1, pp. 93–101.

SUMMERFIELD, P. (1987) 'Cultural reproduction in the education of girls: A study of girls' secondary schooling in two Lancashire towns 1900–50', in HUNT, F. (ed.) *Lessons for Life*, Oxford: Basil Blackwell, pp. 149–70.

SWANN, J. (1992a) 'Ways of speaking', in BONNER, F., GOODMAN, L., ALLEN, R., JANES, L. and KING, C. (eds.) *Imaging Women: Cultural Representations of Gender*, Cambridge: Polity Press, pp. 56–66.

SWANN, J. (1992b) *Girls, Boys and Language*, Oxford: Blackwell.

SWANN, J. (1994) 'What do we do about gender?', in STIERER, B. and MAYBIN, J. (eds.) *Language, Literacy and Learning in Educational Practice*, Clevedon: Multilingual Matters Ltd., pp. 176–87.

SWANN, J. and GRADDOL, D. (1994) 'Gender inequalities in classroom talk', in GRADDOL, D., MAYBIN, J. and STIERER, B. (eds.) *Researching Language and Literacy in Social Context*, Clevedon: Multilingual Matters, pp. 151–67.

TANNEN, D. (1991) *You Just Don't Understand: Women and Men in Conversation*, London: Virago Press.

TEMPLIN, T.J., BRUCE, K. and HART, L. (1988) 'Settling down: An examination of two women physical education teachers', in EVANS, J. (ed.) *Teachers, Teaching and Control in Physical Education*, Lewes: Falmer Press, pp. 57–81.

THE GAY TEACHERS' GROUP (1987) *School's Out: Lesbian and Gay Rights in Education*, London: The Gay Teachers' Group.

THOM, D. (1987) 'Better a teacher than a hairdresser? A mad passion for equality, or, keeping Molly and Betty down', in HUNT, F. (ed.) *Lessons for Life*, Oxford: Basil Blackwell, pp. 124–45.

THOMAS, S. (1991) 'Equality in physical education: A consideration of key issues', in ARMSTRONG, N. and SPARKES, A. (eds.) *Issues in Physical Education*, London: Cassell, pp. 56–73.

THORNE, B. (1993) *Gender Play: Girls and Boys in School*, Buckingham: Open University Press.

TRENCHARD, L. (1984) *Talking about Young Lesbians*, London: London Gay Teenage Group.

TURNBULL, A. (1987) 'Learning her womanly work: The elementary school curriculum 1870–1914', in HUNT, F. (ed.) *Lessons for Life*, Oxford: Basil Blackwell, pp. 83–100.

WAJCMAN, J. (1991) Feminism confronts technology. Paper presented at Gender and Science and Technology 6th International Conference, Australia.

WALDEN, R. and WALKERDINE, V. (1985) *Girls and Mathematics: From Primary to Secondary Schooling*, London: Heinemann.

WALDNER-HAUGRUD, L.K. and MAGRUDER, B. (1996) 'Homosexual identity expression among lesbian and gay adolescents: An analysis of perceived structural associations', *Youth and Society*, **27**, 3, pp. 313–33.

WALKER, J.C. (1988) 'The way men act: Dominant and subordinate male cultures in an inner-city school', *British Journal of Sociology of Education*, **9**, 1, pp. 3–18.

WALKERDINE, V. (1984) 'Developmental psychology and the child-centred pedagogy: The insertion of Piaget into early education', in HENRIQUES, J., HOLLWAY, W., URWIN, C., VENN, C. and WALKERDINE, V. (eds.) *Changing the Subject*, London: Methuen, pp. 153–202.

WALKERDINE, V. (1988) *The Mastery of Reason*, Cambridge: Routledge and Kegan Paul.

WALKERDINE, V. (1989) 'Femininity as performance', *Oxford Review of Education*, **15**, 3, pp. 267–79.

WALKERDINE, V. (1990) *Schoolgirl Fictions*, London: Verso.

WALKERDINE, V. (1993) 'Beyond developmentalism?' *Theory and Psychology*, **3**, 4, pp. 451–69.

WALKERDINE, V. and THE GIRLS AND MATHEMATICS UNIT (1989) *Counting Girls Out*, London: Virago.

WALTER, M. (1987a) 'Generating problems from almost anything, part 1', *Mathematics Teaching*, **120**, September 1987, pp. 2–6.

WALTER, M. (1987b) 'Generating problems from almost anything, part 2', *Mathematics Teaching*, **121**, December 1987, pp. 3–7.

WALTER, M.I. and BROWN, S.I. (1977) 'Problem posing and problem solving: An illustration of their interdependence, *Mathematics Teacher*, January 1977, pp. 4–13.

WARIN, J. (1995) Gender consistency at the start of school. Paper presented at European Conference of Educational Research, University of Bath, September.

WARREN, H. (1984) *Talking about School*, London: London Gay Teenage Group.

WEINER, G. (1994) *Feminisms in Education: An Introduction*, Buckingham: Open University Press.

WEINER, G., ARONT, M. and DAVID, M. (1997) 'Is the future female? Female success, male disadvantage and changing gender patterns in education', in HALSEY, A.H., BROWN, P., LAUDER, H. and STUART-WELLS, A. (eds.) *Education, Culture, Economy, Society*, Oxford: Oxford University Press, pp. 620–30.

WEIR, L. (1994) 'Postmodernising gender: From Adrienne Rich to Judith Butler', in RADTKE, H.L. and STAM, H.J. (eds.) *Power/Gender*, London: Sage, pp. 210–18.

WHITEHEAD, H. (1981) 'The bow and the burden strap: A new look at institutionalised homosexuality in native North America', in ORTNER, S.B. and WHITEHEAD, H. (eds.) *Sexual Meanings: The Cultural Construction of Gender and Sexuality*, Cambridge: Cambridge University Press, pp. 80–115.

WILKINSON, S. and KITZINGER, C. (1993) (eds.) *Heterosexuality: A Feminism and Psychology Reader*, London: Sage.

WILLIAMS, A. (1993) 'Who cares about girls? Equality, physical education and the primary school child', in EVANS, J. (ed.) *Equality, Education and Physical Education*, London: Falmer Press, pp. 125–38.

WILLIS, P. (1977) *Learning to Labour*, Aldershot: Gower Publishing Company.

WILLOTT, S. and GRIFFIN, C. (1996) 'Men, masculinity and the challenge of long-term unemployment', in MAC AN GHAILL, M. (ed.) *Understanding Masculinities: Social Relations and Cultural Arenas*, Buckingham: Open University Press, pp. 77–92.

WILSON, A. (1996) 'How we find ourselves: Identity development and two-spirit people', *Harvard Educational Review*, **66**, 2, pp. 303–17.

WITTGENSTEIN, L. (1922) *Tractatus Logico-Philosophicus*, London: Routledge and Kegan Paul.

WOLLFENSPERGER, J. (1993) 'Science is truly a male world. The interconnectedness of knowledge, gender and power within university education', *Gender and Education*, **5**, 1, pp. 37–54.

WOOLF, V. (1938) *Three Guineas*, Harmondsworth, Middlesex: Penguin Books.

YOUNG, I.M. (1990) 'The ideal of community and the politics of difference', in NICHOLSON, L.J. (ed.) *Feminism/Postmodernism*, London: Routledge, pp. 300–23.

YOUNG, I.M. (1994) 'Gender as sexuality: Thinking about women as a social collectivity', *Signs*, **19**, 3, pp. 713–38.

Index

abortion 73
abuse 24, 103
achievement 1, 20, 31–3, 54, 96, 98
adolescence 16, 23, 29, 45, 69–70
   masculinity 96
   relationships 105
   sport 99
   stereotypes 76, 115
   teachers 116
advertising 16
agenda-setting 5
Akanke 105
androcentrism 6, 39, 41, 47, 49
androgen-insensitivity syndrome 42–3
Anstiss, J. 21, 27
appearance 16, 27
Appleby, Y. 106
art 10
assessment 31–3, 54
Assessment of Performance Unit 28
assignment of gender 39, 42, 44, 47
assumptions 2, 6, 38, 39
   biological sex 40
   empowerment 68
   gender 46, 54–5
   heterosexuality 116
   ideology 69
   mathematics 77
   stereotypes 57
attachment 73
Attanucci, J. 73–4
Attar, D. 29
attribution of gender 39–40, 49
avoidance behaviour 23

barbarians 19, 34
behaviour 39, 44, 45–6, 50, 58, 61
beliefs 45
Bem, S.L. 39

berdache 47
Berger, J. 10, 49
bias 33, 35, 74
biology 38–43, 46–8
Boaler, J. 76
bodybuilding 101–2
Boer War 82
Boldt, G.M. 50
bourgeoisie 83
breastfeeding 12
Brown, L.M. 69
Brown, S.I. 77
bullying 22–3, 96, 97
Burchell, H. 34–5
Burman, E. 59–60
Butler, J. 49, 51

camaraderie 24
care orientation 73
Carrington, B. 87–8
Carroll, B. 29
Cassatt, M. 10
child-centred ideology 45, 59
childbearing 12
childcare manuals 59
Chodorow, N.J. 73, 75
chromosomes 41–2, 44
civilization 19, 30, 34
classical studies 35
classrooms 24–5, 110–11
co-operation 25
Coles, F. 101
collaboration 25
collation 109–10
competition 20, 25, 29–30, 104
comprehensive schools 86
computers 21, 35, 112–13
Connell, R.W. 40
contact sports 101

contextual issues 76
Crozier, J. 21, 27
culture
  achievement 98
  androcentrism 41
  comparisons 6–7
  computers 35
  construction 35
  differences 14
  dominance 68
  games-playing 21
  gender construction 38–53
  homophobia 103
  popular 16
  sexual harassment 23
  sports 97
curriculum 3, 12–13, 68, 80–92
  homophobia 104
  masculinity 96
  materials 110
  secondary 20
  status 85
  subject takeup 29

dance 101, 113
Darwin, C. 7
Davies, B. 46, 49–50
de-posing of problems 76–7
deconstruction 2–3, 38, 58, 113–14, 117
decontextualized knowledge 15, 64–6,
  76–8
deficit models 20, 34–5, 54
Degas, E. 10
degendering 15
Delamont, S. 35
demonstrations 21
design and technology 81–2, 85–9
develpmental psychology 58–9, 74
deviance 27, 47, 96
Dewar, A. 101
dimorphism 46–8, 51
disabilities 106
discourse 5–6, 9, 34, 65–6
  deconstruction 58
  definition 2–3
  development 60
  empowerment 66–71
discrimination 20, 33

disruptive behaviour 21–2
docile bodies 3
domestic science 13
Dominican Republic 47
Draper, J. 20, 23
dress 22, 23
dualism 8, 39, 40, 45
Dugan, K.B. 23
Duncan, J. 6–7, 8
Duveen, G. 44

education
  females 11–16
  gender issues 54–63
  problem-solving 75–8
Education Acts 85
Ehrhardt, A.A. 43
elementary schools 22, 83, 85–6
elitism 82
Ellsworth, E. 68, 69
embryos 41
empowerment 66–71
Enlightenment 9, 117
Epstein, D. 104
equality 80–92
equipment 20–1
ethics 14, 74
ethnicity 33, 70, 88, 95–7, 105–6
Euclid 77
evolutionary theory 6–7
examinations 31–3, 61, 87–8
expectations 29, 35
extra-curricular activities 21, 99
eye contact 21

fantasy play 26
Fausto-Sterling, A. 41–2
feelings 39, 116
female voices 64–79
femininities 4–5, 20, 29, 39
  attachment 73
  curriculum 89
  gender roles 48
  mathematics 66
  secondary schools 93–108
  stereotypes 57
feminism 1, 8, 68, 74, 99
fictive kinship 70

Fisher, J. 24–5
Fletcher, S. 12
Fordham, S. 70
Foucault, M. 55–7, 64
Francis, B. 20
Freud, S. 41
friendships 22
funding 81

Gatens, M. 9
gay men 4, 8, 51, 103–6
gaze 9–11, 15–16, 22
    classroom talks 25
    dance 101
    gender roles 51
    normalizing 58
gender 9, 11–12, 15, 29
    curriculum 80
    development 71–5
    differences 19–37
    education 54–63
    monitoring 109–11
    social construction 3, 38–53
    subject takeup 27–31
genitalia 42–4, 46–8
Gilligan, C. 14–15, 69, 71–5
Gipps, C. 32, 61
Giroux, H.A. 67, 68–9
glass ceilings 1
Graddol, D. 24, 25
graduate schools 23
grammar schools 85
Gramsci, A. 2
Griffin, P. 101
Griffiths, M. 35

harassment 22–3
headteachers 57
health, 12, 82
health visitors 58
Hearn, J. 98
Hechman, S.J. 74
hegemony 6, 54, 64
    definition 2–3
    disciplines 91
    marginalization 94
    masculinity 96–8, 102, 115–16
    norms 78

heterosexuality 50–1, 59, 93, 98, 102, 116
hierarchies of oppression 69
higher education 19, 28, 98
historical issues 11–14, 82–9
Hohnston, L. 101
home economics 28–9, 85, 88
homophobia 101, 103
homosexuality 50–1, 94, 103–6
hooks, b. 96
hormones 41–3
housewifery 13
hypermasculinities 95, 97

identities 5, 8, 38
    gender 39–40, 43, 43–5, 47, 49
    masculinity 76
    sexuality 103
    society 46
    subject takeup 29
ideology 82–4
Imperato-McGinley, J. 47
imperialism 7
Impressionism 10
in-groups 5–6
information technology 27
International Amateur Athletic
    Federation 43
Internet 112–13
interpersonal relations 14–15, 19, 35, 57

Johnson, R. 104
joking 24
Jones, A. 28
justice 14, 71–4, 76

Kant, I. 71
Kessler, S. 39–40, 43, 48–50, 96
Key Stage tests 20, 32
Kirk, C.M. 28
Kitzinger, C. 70
Klobukowska, E. 43
knowledge 9–14, 19, 27, 64–6, 97
Kohlberg, L. 14, 71–2, 76–7

labelling 16, 44
laboratories 20
Landau, N.R. 28, 30

language 6, 11, 15–16, 24, 41
    classroom talk 24–5
    sociolinguistics 74–5
lavatories 22, 57
learning child 57–61
learning preferences 76
Lee, V.E. 23
Lees, S. 16
leisure facilities 29
Lenskyj, J. 101
lesbians 4, 7–8, 51, 101, 103–6
life in school 20–7
Lloyd, B. 44
Luke, C. 24
Lukes, S. 3

Mac an Ghaill, M. 51, 96
macho males 93
McKenna, W. 39–40, 43, 48–50
marginalization 81–2
male domination 20–7
malnutrition 82
Manet, E. 10–11
Manthorpe, C. 90
manual labour 83, 97
marginalization 3–4, 25–6
    hegemony 94
    homophobia 104
    lesbians 101
    sports 96
marriage 13
Marxism 2
masculinities 3, 5, 29, 35, 39
    curriculum 89
    gender roles 48
    hegemony 115–16
    identities 76
    mathematics 66
    performance 40
    resistance 88
    secondary schools 93–108
    stereotypes 57
    Subject 71
    working class 84
Massey, D. 35
mathematics 15, 20, 28, 30, 65–6, 78
    competition 30
    examinations 31–2

primary 34
problem-solving 75–7
teachers 32–3
media 95
meetings 27
micro-powers 56
micro-resistances 56
mind/body dichotomy 8–9
misogyny 95, 99
mixed schools 28
Money, J. 43
monitoring 109–11
moral development 14, 14–15, 65, 71–5
moral philosophy 73
Morgan, E. 6
motherhood 58–9
Mullerian Inhibitory Factor 41, 42
multiple-choice questions 32
Murphy, P. 32, 61, 76
Myers, D.J. 23

name-calling 21–2, 103
national curriculum 15, 81–2, 87
nature 9
Netherlands 28
neuroscience 46
New Zealand 28
non-macho males 4
normalizing gaze 58
nursery schools 23–4, 26

Ohrn, E. 19
Orbach, S. 98
Osborne, J. 15
Other 3, 5–18, 34–5
    curriculum 80–92
    exclusion 35
    masculinities 94–5
    school 19
out-groups 5–6

parallel others 89–91
Parker, A. 104
patriarchy 20
pedagogy 57–61, 67–8
peer groups 28, 45, 98
Peters, R.S. 19
philosophy 8–9, 14, 71, 73, 74

physical characteristics 39
physical education 13, 27, 29, 81–2,
    84–9, 96
  deconstruction 113–14
  subordination 100–2, 105
physical harassment 22–3
physics 15, 28, 29
Piaget, J. 34, 60, 71
play 60
polarization 39
Pollock, G. 10–11
poverty 82, 84
power relations 3, 5–6, 38, 45
  abuse 104
  art 11
  challenge 116
  change 98
  deconstruction 117
  gaze 9–11
  gender 55–7, 57–61
  language 65
  reason 66–71
  resistance 26, 27
  roles 48–51
  schools 19
  sociolinguistics 74
  space 111–13
pressurization 30
prestige 30
primary schools 19–20, 30, 34,
    54
  classroom talks 24–5
  specialization 80–1
  sports 99
  stereotypes 116
privilege 22
problem-solving 75–8
psychology 74
Pyke, K.D. 95

qualifications 33
quantitative evidence 109–10

racism 70, 95, 105–6
Randall, G.J. 21
rationalism 68, 74
Rawls, J. 71
re-posing of problems 76–7

reason 14–15, 20, 64–75
reconceptualisation of gender issues
    54–63
Records of Achievement 34–5
recreational areas 22
reproduction 12–13, 101
reputations 16
research 20, 25, 32–3, 40–1, 72
resistance 26–7, 56, 61, 88, 99
resources 20
responsibilities 73
Riddell, S. 21, 24, 29, 86
Robinson, K.H. 26
Rogers, C. 67
Rogers, M. 105
roles 39–40, 43–5, 48–50
rote learning 66
Rousseau, J-J. 12

Said, E.W. 7
scapegoats 95
scholarships 31
schools
  curriculum 80–92
  gender differences 19–37
  homosexuality 103–6
  life 20–7
  power relations 56–7
  sports 100–1
science 2, 15, 20–1, 28, 35, 64
  contextual issues 76
  curriculum 89–90
  performance 35
  problem-solving 75
secondary modern schools 85–6
secondary schools 13, 19–20, 22, 34,
    54, 61
  homophobia 103
  masculinities 93–108
  specialization 80–1
  subject takeup 27–31
self-evident truths 2
service ideology 13
sex
  biology 40–3
  definition 38–9
sexism 16, 29, 68–9, 95
sexual harassment 23–4, 112–13

sexuality 10, 13, 16, 27, 57, 81
  homophobia 103
  lesbians 106
  sport 99–100
Shilling, C. 20, 49
single-sex schools 28
sixth-form colleges 30
Smith, C. 44
social construction of gender 3, 38–53
social construction of masculinities
    93–4
social control 16, 82–4
social roles 2, 12–13, 15, 26
social sciences 28
society 45–51
sociolinguistics 74
space 20–4, 26, 56–7, 111–13
Sparkes, A. 89, 101
specialization 80
Spencer 7
sports 22, 29–30, 88, 96–7
  competition 104
  deconstruction 113–14
sporty girls 4, 99–103
Stables, A. 28
staffrooms 24, 111–12
stages of moral development 14, 71–2
status 85–9, 90
stereotypes 27–9, 33, 44–6, 49
  adolescence 76, 115
  gender roles 50–1
  homophobia 103, 104
  macho males 93
  masculinities 57
  sporty girls 99, 100
sterility 12
stigmatization 97, 103
strategies 109–14
streaming 85, 96
Subject 5–6, 8, 15, 16
  curriculum 80–92
  girls' schooling 34
  masculinities 71
subject ideologies 82–4
subordination 93–108
subservience 12
Summerfield, P. 13
surveillance 57, 58, 59

Swann, J. 24, 25
symbolism 15

takeup of subjects 27–31
Tannen, D. 74–6
teachers
  adolescence 116
  attention 21–2
  beliefs 45
  bullying 97
  classroom talks 25
  empowerment 67–8
  expectations 29
  feminism 68
  gender 19
  girls' schooling 34–5
  homophobia 103, 104–5
  ideology 58
  impersonal relations 20
  mathematics 32–3
  physical education 102–3
  power 57
  pressurization 30–1
  resistance 26–7
  science 90
  sexual harassment 23–4
  training 82
team sports 22
technology 15
testing 32–3
textbooks 28
Thorne, B. 22, 98
time 20–4, 26, 56–7
toolkit 109–14
traditional gender monitoring 109–11
transsexuals 40, 42, 47, 50
truth 2, 10

unemployment 97
United States of America 11, 22–3, 31,
    90, 96, 101
university places 31

values 14, 38, 83
verbal harassment 22–3
violence 96
virtual space 112–13
vocational qualifications 33

vocations 13
voices 64–79, 80–92
voyeurism 10

Wajcman, J. 15
Walden, R. 34
Walker, J.C. 96–7
Walkerdine, V. 23, 26, 34, 64–6
Walter, M. 77
Weiner, G. 5, 12
welfare state 57

what-if-not 113–14
Whitehead, H. 47
Wittig 51
Wolffensperger, J. 28
woman as Other 7–11
Wood, E. 88
work 60
working class 82–4
workshops 20

Young, I.M. 50